Imagine, Believe & Prosper

Imagine, Believe & Prosper

A GUIDE TO FINANCIAL SUCCESS

Gloria S. Riley

ISBN 979-8-9886760-0-3

Published by Gloria S. Riley

Printed in the United States of America

Dedication

I dedicate this book to my loving husband, Ellis, and sons, Caland, Jolin, and Zarren, for their never-ending encouragement and support of all my endeavors to live life to its fullest. I could live a life of gardening and enjoying the beach, including yoga practice and spa days, but why when I can have it all?

Table of Contents

Introduction

As an insurance agent, agency owner, and finance coach, I have met people from all occupations and socioeconomic statuses, and they all have one thing in common—the need for and use of money for goods and services. Some are in the beginning stages of acquiring money by investing; others are in the planning phase; some are in the accumulation phase of building a portfolio of assets; and lastly, others have evolved to the end stage, the distribution phase, which leads to retirement and their pot of gold. And at each of those phases, we tend to get stuck and need help advancing.

While authoring this book, I would often reflect on my experiences growing up when my beloved aunt and guardian's home foreclosed due to her illness, and the lack of adequate disability insurance and resources needed to save our home made me feel. The many clients I have helped by putting plans in place in case the unexpected happens; they would have the risk covered. I am grateful to be able to assist clients with achieving their goals and share in their successes. The wealth of knowledge and experience I have acquired and applied to my life and now may share with many is my honor. I know what I discuss in this book is life-changing, and I cannot wait to hear your testimonies.

I found similarities in my life as an entrepreneur, desiring and seeking more excellent knowledge to assist on the financial success journey. Like most entrepreneurial personalities I have known, I bumped my head a couple of times, experienced burnout, dusted myself off, and kept moving toward my comeback. At times I didn't know which path to take, the time required to reach a specific goal, how I would feel during the journey, or how the results would look, but it always made me happy knowing change was coming. I call it my belief factor. After all, we are destined for success and strive to better ourselves by making our dreams a reality. And, like most, that was enough for me to believe, or, better said, to Imagine, Believe & Prosper ®.

This mantra keeps me driven, inspired, and committed to reaching my life goals.

How to Read This Book

Imagine, Believe & Prosper: A Guide to Financial Success provides valuable information, simple lessons, and personal experiences I have gained. You will also find information shared with me that I now share with you. Over the years, I searched for tools, associations, resources, and directions to improve my situation. The information I have gathered and impart to you here would have benefited me years ago. The great news is that you and your loved ones can benefit from this information today.

To make this information easiest to learn and apply, this book is divided into four parts that cover the different aspects of growing wealth. They include:

Part I: Success and Mindset

Success can be defined in many ways depending on the individual's goals and aspirations. Success is often associated with achieving a desire outcome, reaching a certain level of status or accomplishment, or fulfilling one's potential. It can be measured in terms of wealth, recognition, personal fulfillment, or any number of other metrics.

Mindset, on the other hand, refers to a person's attitude, beliefs, and mindset that influence their thoughts, actions, and behaviors. Mindset is the way we think about ourselves, our abilities, and our potential. It can be influenced by past experiences, social and cultural factors, and personal beliefs and values.

Part II: Financial Planning

Financial Planning is the process of developing a strategy to manage one's finances and achieve specific financial goals. This typically involves creating a budget, investing money in different financial instruments, managing debt, and planning for retirement and other long-term financial goals. Financial planning often involves working with a financial advisor or planner who can help individuals create a personalized plan based on their specific financial situation, goals, and risk tolerance. A financial planner can provide guidance and advice on how to manage one's money and investments to help achieve financial security and meet financial objectives.

Part III: Abundance and Mindset

Abundance refers to a mindset and belief that there are enough resources, opportunities, and prosperity to go around. It's a perspective that focuses on the positive aspects of life and the belief that there is enough for everyone, including oneself. Abundance is often associated with financial abundance or wealth, but it can also refer to an abundance of love, health, happiness, and other positive qualities.

In short, abundance and mindset are interconnected, and cultivating an abundance mindset can help us recognize and appreciate the abundance in our lives, attract more positivity and abundance, and approach life with a positive, growth-oriented attitude.

Part IV: Diversification

Diversification is an investment strategy that involves spreading out investments among s different assets or securities to reduce risk and increase potential returns. This strategy is based on the idea that by investing in a variety of assets, one can reduce the impact of individual asset performance on the overall portfolio performance. Overall, diversification is a fundamental strategy for managing investment risk and maximizing returns over the long term.

Each chapter is full of information on how to prepare to receive your wealth.

Who This Book is For

This writing is personal in that I genuinely want to assist everyone who reads it to acquire exactly what he/she needs or desires and grow financially and personally. Personal development excites me because there is always room for improvement, and there is something new to learn daily. Stretching yourself from where you are to where you want to be will cause you to reach another dimension, which is your maximum potential. I learned about the stretching philosophy from one of my mentors, John C Maxwell. He teaches on the Law of the Rubber Band and points out the only use of a rubber band comes when it is stretched. The rubber band must be pulled to give value and to be useful. Similarly, people must be stretched to maximize their gifts and talents. It is important to associate with people who will stretch you.

I hope that the information ahead will provide valuable information in assisting to maximize your financial security. You are reading this book because you know you are destined for success, can benefit from more motivation and direction, and desire to implement new plans to realize your dream goals. Books and life are meant for enjoyment and to share with others so that they too may benefit from the joy, happiness, creativity, adventure, and success that results from applying the rule of stretching.

Therefore, I intend to assist you to get to the place you need to be by becoming the person you are destined to become. I want you to be a financially sound and responsible person by setting goals, monitoring spending, minimizing debt, budgeting, possessing the correct mindset, having an abundant attitude while steadily saving for a secure retirement, and giving to others in need.

It is my aspiration that you are financially secure every single day, have peace of mind, and not worry about money or your essential needs. I hope that you have sufficient income to cover expenses and have savings to cover emergencies with proper planning and a financial mindset. My hopes as an author are that I have impelled you to achieve the success you so richly deserve and that you acknowledge that you must give a final accounting of what you did with the gifts, talents, and abilities given to you from the Creator.

PART I:
SUCCESS AND MINDSET

What you imagine and desire to possess in your life is powerful when you put this knowledge to effective use. Turn these thoughts into actionable steps and strategies to improve your current situation. You must have the proper mindset to advance your dreams by focusing, setting goals, creating systems for success, generously giving to others, and sticking to your plan. These chapters will help prepare you for your next destination to financial success.

CHAPTER 1

Achieve Your Desires

Every thought, hunch, or inclination begins with a dream. But we often don't give those desires the weight they deserve, and we let them get lost in the shuffle of life. Looking at other people who are succeeding, success might seem like a combination of good fortune and genetics. That is not true. You can be just as successful as anyone else. You just need to do the same things those successful people are doing before each leap they take.

To achieve your desires, there's a process to follow: 1) Define your desire 2) Take action, and 3) Manifestation. This chapter is about Defining your desire, and the next few chapters in Part I cover Taking action and Manifesting.

If we're going to move forward and achieve our goals, we must identify our desires first so we can choose the most helpful actions to take that will bring about the reality we wish to create for ourselves and our loved ones. See there? It just takes a few tips to make the leap from mediocrity to superstar status. The differences between remarkable success and average results are real--but smaller than you might think.

For instance, a young couple, Robert and Carolyn, consulted me because their budget was off track; they were overspending. Before getting married, both had taken out a lot of student loans. Both were college graduates. It became clear to me that he had a history of regularly contributing to a savings account, and she had high credit card balances on clothing, travel, and entertainment. Once they were married, they took lavish trips, it seemed to me because Robert wanted to impress Carolyn.

"Did you still find a way to save *some* money?" I asked.

Bob looked at the rug in the center of my office. "No," he said.

Even worse, the year before they moved out of an apartment into a nice community where they purchased a home. Why did I say, 'even worse?' Well, because they incurred a higher fixed debt with the mortgage and both student loans. The mortgage payment was more than their old rental payment. As a solution they refinanced their mortgage to bring those payments down, but all they did with that extra money is spend it on a trip to Europe.

"I don't understand," Carolyn said. "We have college friends who take amazing trips and have fabulous homes. Their jobs aren't that different from ours. What are we doing wrong?"

"I really want to help you," I said. "We can create budgets all day long, but that won't help you if whatever budget you walk out of here with isn't working toward what you really desire in life."

"Wow, our other finance coach never asked us about what we want, "Carolyn said.

After some discussion, they decided what they really wanted was to change careers. This would mean lower salaries as they entered different industries and maybe taking an internship along the way.

"But if we go for our dreams, we'll lose our house, won't we?" Robert asked. He had a panicked look on his face.

"Not necessarily," I said. We created a budget for them to pay their fixed monthly fees, along with necessities. But they had to commit to no travel for two years. Not spending that money would allow them to take the salary cuts until they could increase their incomes and have a healthy savings.

"I really don't want to quit the country club," Carolyn said. "But I do want to put my heart and soul into urban planning instead of selling insurance."

With their desires clear, we were able to create that budget they would follow. And in a few years and promotions, they took another fancy trip—and they paid for it with their bank cards, not on credit. Whatever you desire, you can take the same steps as Robert and Carolyn to achieve your dreams.

The story's moral is that you must analyze your desires alongside your finances. Forecast your future income with salary increases and review your budget regularly. Living within your budget should outweigh any other goals because otherwise, you're always playing catch-up and not getting anywhere. I bet your desire isn't to live a stressful life. So, live below your means, and don't feel pressured to make all the decisions now because you are 'living for today, like tomorrow will not be there.' Many younger couples feel they need to live for today, and tomorrow is not promised. But choose to believe that you will have the desires of your heart, but you must have a budget and a financial plan and take the action steps to bring it into reality.

Often, I think about the young couples like Robert and Carolyn I have helped, whether they were newlyweds or starting a career. We always begin with *defining* what your goals and values are. Ask yourself:

- What is important to you?
- What do you want to achieve?
- How much income do you want when you retire?
- How do you want to invest?

All these questions are important in defining your desire so you can achieve it. As you develop a good picture of your desire, keep it in your foremost thoughts. One way I do this for myself and suggest to my clients is to create affirmations around your desires.

AFFIRMATIONS FOR SUCCESS

The path toward financial freedom—or whatever you desire—starts and ends with you. You must recite, imagine, and believe in your dreams to realize them. Anything you desire is easier to achieve when your mindset is in sync with that outcome. You must also commit to the actions toward manifesting this desire.

Think about it. If you have a dream of financial freedom but you don't believe it's possible and can't imagine yourself living that life—are you likely to do the work? Probably not. And even if you do take some action, will you put your heart into it and be consistent? Probably not. You'll be expecting to fail to prove yourself right that your dream wasn't possible. This had happened when Carolyn and Robert tried to save in the past.

Or you can train your mind to be your ally in creating your financial freedom.

I find that creating and repeating affirmations work well in adjusting my mind to commit to making a big change. Affirmations are statements in the positive, as if what you want in the future is already yours in the present. Follow them up with a few actions you are committing to take to behave as if those desires are true (and to get closer to achieving them).

Affirmations often directly contradict your negative beliefs or doubts. For instance, Carolyn had believed, "I can't save money." So, she changed it to "I'm great at saving money." And whereas before she bought things without thinking about the budget, she committed to the action, "I only buy what I need and only pay with cash. I don't have the cash; I don't buy it." Robert's shift was tough, too. He went from believing, "I am only worthy of my wife if I can give her whatever she wants," to "I am worthy of Susan's love because I am a loving husband." He had to go from always saying 'yes' to his wife to make her happy regardless of what they could afford to saying 'no' to her so they could stay on their path toward their desires.

Your affirmations may not feel true today, but when you repeat them to yourself every day, they become your new truth about yourself and your life. Below are some examples of affirmations for financial freedom desires. With each affirmation I share an action or two that will support this new truth about myself.

1. I Tread the Path to Financial Freedom

One of my main goals in life is achieving financial freedom. I excitedly look forward to the day when I have all my finances under full control.

2. Each Day Brings a New Opportunity to Make Responsible Decisions About Money

I treat financial wellness with the same importance as other daily priorities. I structure cues to remind me that I am committed to being a wise spender and saver. My main cue is to weigh whether something is a want or need. Before spending a cent, I ask myself questions about the purpose of the purchase.

When I determine that something is a want, I avoid making the purchase. I know that it is important to make myself happy, but I also know that something for my happiness still has the same effect when I purchase it later.

3. I am Also Committed to Only Acquiring What I Can Buy with Cash

The credit monster is my greatest adversary. I avoid using credit cards when I am unable to repay them.

4. I Ensure I clear My Debt Each Month so I Maintain a Good Credit Score

This approach makes me eligible for significant provisions like a mortgage or my kids' education. Today, I acknowledge that the path to financial freedom is sometimes challenging but I am dedicated to keeping it as smooth as possible. My strategies for staying on the right side of debt are effective enough to guide me.

You can be as successful as you want to be. Anything you desire is at your fingertips, but you must be willing to change your beliefs and actions to change your life. Don't rely on luck or an idyllic past for success. You already have everything you need. Create your own daily affirmations that support your desires and what you want to believe to be true, and the rewards are sure to follow.

Here are some journaling prompts for you to reflect on what you want most in life:

1.

1. What are my desires and dreams?

2. What negative beliefs do I have about what I want for myself? What actions am I taking that are working against creating the life I desire?

3. For each negative belief you list, write it in the positive. For example, "I can't save money," might become, "I can save money." Do the same for the unhelpful actions you listed above. "I buy things I can't afford on credit cards," might shift to, "I only purchase things I can pay cash for."

CHAPTER 2

Goal Setting for Success

A lot of people talk about what they are going to be, but only a handful of people talk about how they are going to achieve it. Be honest. Are you one of the people who have big dreams but are unable to take the first step toward them? Every day is a new day, but if we don't have a dream or don't have a plan to get there, our days will be as dull as dishwater. All the time we spend reminiscing about our past, we are wasting the limited time we have to make our dreams a reality. No matter what you feel you haven't accomplished so far, today you can decide to take a different path and join the people who are achieving their desires.

In the last chapter we got noticeably clear on your dreams, and in the affirmations exercise, you might have noticed having to come up with the actions that would support those desires. Now we're taking a closer look at how to choose the right actions toward specific goals. Let's find out what you'll do to set yourself up for success and create the dreams you imagined for yourself in Chapter 1.

Our dreams or desires are destinations (or manifestations) that we can travel to when we set the right goals and take positive action to get us closer. A *goal* is a short step in your journey of success, and the compilation of such goals will result in your being able to see the finish line.

A note of warning: Keep your eyes on yourself. One person's goals will differ from another's. Some of us might have big goals, and some of us might have small goals. If you want to go back to graduate school, that desire becomes more possible when you complete a series of big goals like taking required tests, completing the application, applying for funding, etc. For where you may be today, the goal might make the most sense for you could be smaller, like researching colleges and programs to choose the ones you'd like to attend.

Now, the secret ingredient that you need to finish this race and make your dream a reality is 'Passion.' From time to time, we may feel a disconnection between what we are doing and what we want and value. Such a disconnection happens due to a lack of transparency of what we want in life. This is where passion kicks in to add a twist to our journey toward success. Even if we take a piece of paper and jot down all the goals we want to achieve, without the passion to execute them, our goals will be words only. Yes, of course you need to keep a record of all your goals in writing, but if you do not have the motivation or passion to execute them you will not move forward in life. You'll have passion to achieve the goals that lead to your desire.

Your passion is the driving force of your path to success. It also holds the dominant position in your thoughts, actions, and conversations. For instance, maybe you have a big goal in life, you can't stop talking about it, thinking about it, and doing things that make progress—you are passion-driven. But, if you dim your passion and keep that dream on the shelf where it gathers dust, all the paths leading to that success will stay hidden, perhaps right in front of you. So, harness your passion and pour it into the goals you set in this chapter because then you'll do everything it takes to achieve them.

Okay, hang on a minute. That's right you need to *set* your goals to achieve them. You cannot simply sit in bed and think to yourself "I want it" and expect your desire to happen instantly. Goal setting is a step-by-step process that starts with what you want to achieve and ends with your working hard to achieve it. Below I outline the Five Steps to Set Your Goals.

1. Choose goals that motivate you.

If there is no motivation or passion, you will never be able to achieve your desires.

2. Always set SMART goals.

I am sure some of you have heard of SMART in a professional context, but the real question is—have you applied it to your day-to-day activities? For my readers who are not aware, SMART, stands for:

Specific: What exactly do you want to accomplish?

Measurable: How will you make progress and know if you're on track or not?

Attainable: Is it reasonable to accomplish this desired outcome?

Relevant: Does this goal make sense with your larger desires and dreams?

Time-bound: When do you expect to finish this goal?

When your goals fit these criteria, you'll be able to plan the necessary actions you'll complete in a timely manner.

3. Always put your goal in writing.

Write your goals down and keep track of them.

Small tip—Always use the word, "will" instead of "might/would like to," since "I might buy a yacht" lacks passion and gives you a lethargic feeling compared to "I will buy a yacht."

4. Create an action plan.

Now you're ready for the fourth step: There will be a series of specific steps along the way to achieve your specific goal. Having a step-by-step plan will make you feel confident and give you a taste of victory as well as you move from one step to the next.

5. Follow the plan and achieve it.

None of this will be a reality unless you work hard and stick to your plan because, in the end, arduous work pays off.

Some examples of goal setting are saving money to purchase a vehicle or a home, funding a college education, going on your dream vacation, or opening your own business.

Set Your Goals

"Careful planning puts you ahead in the long run; when you hurry and scurry it puts you further behind at a loss" Proverbs 21:5.

The Word of God informs us that planning for our future will produce success. The question is how to start. We start with short-term objectives to reach long-term goals. In this section I have a series of exercises for you to create both kinds of goals for yourself.

First, recognize that there will be short-term objectives, which are the small steps on the path to reach a long-term goal. Just like your goals, good objectives will fit the SMART criteria and be (mostly) measurable and specific steps, actions, and tasks necessary to achieve or accomplish a goal (s). Goals and objectives are proportionate to each other, so a monthly goal will have weekly and/or daily objectives. A yearly goal will have monthly objectives, and so forth. Your success depends on setting these goals and objectives in the different areas of your life from finance and work to health and relationships--even charitable giving.

Feeling a little lost? I was, too, when I first learned how dreams and desires, goals, and objectives all fit together. This became clearer after I became a John Maxwell certified speaker. One thing I learned from him is the step-by-step process below:

- Recognize your *dreams* and write them down.
- Recognize where you are so that you can identify where you should go.
- Write a statement of purpose that reflects your dreams.
- Write your *goals* based on your dream.
- Move into action by planning your *objectives*.
- Be ready to adjust your actions.
- As you accomplish your objectives... celebrate!

When you bring boundless passion to these steps, you'll be celebrating every big and small win you have along the way. This keeps you motivated to keep acting and follow the course you've laid out for yourself to arrive at your dreams.

Feel ready to start setting some goals? I believe you are. Let's get started with the goals worksheets in the next chapter.

CHAPTER 3

Set Your Goals

Is the path from your desires to the actions you'll take making more sense now? I hope so. Sometimes doing is the best way to learn, so let's get to the good stuff and start planning your success. Answer the following prompts to create your Daily, Weekly, Monthly, and Yearly plan. Along the way you'll see Bible verses to encourage you to keep going. As you do so, keep in mind everything you learned about creating SMART goals in the last chapter.

"Write down this vision; inscribe it on tablets so one may easily read it." Habakkuk 2.2

This Daily, Weekly, Monthly, and Yearly plan will help you write your map from where you are now to where and what you would like to do in five years. Set your five-year goal(s) in the first blank below. Then work backward with the Daily, then Monthly exercises to set your objectives and goals to get you to this five-year dream. And don't forget to set your Personal Finance Goals at the end. This will give you a head start on PART II and assist you in thinking about your Five-Year Goal.

Five-Year Goal: _____

DAILY

Write down what you want to accomplish for the day.

_____

_____

_____

What steps do you need to take to complete your objective?

_____

_____

Monitor if you have given yourself enough time; if not, readjust for the next time you have this task.

_____

_____

Were you able to reach your daily goal? How do you know?

_____

_____

WEEKLY

This section is short because no matter what your other goals are, this one is about

staying organized and committed.

- Once a week, review your daily goals from the week before.
- Which ones need to be carried over? Add them to your daily goals for this coming week.
- Which ones need to be changed or shifted? Make those adjustments accordingly.
- Measure if you seem on track with day-to-day actions toward reaching your Monthly Goals.
- Find at least five things to celebrate.

MONTHLY GOALS

"Where there is no vision, the people cast off restraint; but happy is he that keeps the law" Proverbs 29:18.

- Set aside time to review and revamp the budget.
- Create/write objectives to reach your 5-year goal.

What did I accomplish?

_____

What is visible to let me know I have reached my goals?

_____

_____

Decide and write what should be worked on during the upcoming month.

_____

_____

_____

Were my goals reachable? How do I know?

_____

_____

Did I reach them in a timely fashion?

_____

Did I have to make any readjustments?

_____

I Can I celebrate?

_____

"Take delight in the Lord, and he will give you the desires of your heart" Psalm 37:4.

_____

YEARLY

- Set aside time to completely revamp the budget.
- Go through your journal; make note of the smaller goals you listed and how they might cor relate to your overall five-year goal.

Make certain that you have created/written an objective to reach your 5-year goal.

_____

What did I accomplish?

_____

What is visible to let me know that I have reached my goals?

_____

_____

Decide and write what should be worked on during the upcoming months.

_____

_____

_____

Were my goals reachable? How do I know?

_____

_____

Did I reach them in a timely fashion?

_____

Did I have to make any readjustments?

_____

Can I celebrate?

_____

_____

"The rich rules over the poor, and the borrower is servant to the lender." Proverbs 22:7.

_____

Debt (a liability or obligation to pay)

List the order in which you want to pay off debts:

Creditors	Amount
_____	_____
_____	_____
_____	_____
_____	_____

PERSONAL FINANCE GOALS

"Suppose one of you wants to built a tower. Won't you first sit down and estimate the cost to see is you have enough money to complete it?" Luke 14:28

_____

Educational Goals:

Individual whose education I will fund:

Person	School	Annual Cost	Total Cost

"But as for you, be strong and do not give up, for your work will rewarded."

2 Chonicles 15:7

Lifestyle Goals:

I intend to make the following major purchases (home, business, automobile, travel, etc.)

Item	Time Frame	Amount

I intend to achieve the following income of $ _____

Saving and investing goals:

I intend to save _____ of my income annually.

Other saving goals are _____

I intend to make the following investments:

Item	Time Frame	Amount

CHAPTER 4
Success Habit Tips

Achieving your goals builds your self-confidence and brings feelings of success and happiness. This begins as you make progress with daily goals and objectives and increases as you complete longer-term actions and outcomes. However, I have seen my clients become overwhelmed by scary, big goals and dreams and want to give up on their daily action steps. When that happens, we get back to basics and focus on the daily activities or habits they can commit to.

Robert and Carolyn didn't go from overspending to saving wisely overnight. Some of their first daily actions included: skipping lattes on the drive to work, cooking meals at home, and living with basic cable. A few times they ordered dinner, and Robert upgraded the cable to watch sports for a month, but in time they found their new normal. That's because your daily actions, repeated over and over, become habits. It became normal to carry a thermos of coffee to work, and they started enjoying time together in the kitchen. Robert's brother invited him for game days. And guess what? The couple wasn't miserable at all. They were happier than when they were always jetting to someplace and looking for the next thing to buy.

Thankfully, you can easily establish daily habits that bring you the success you desire. Those regular objectives you set for yourself will become reflexive choices you don't think about—the more you do them consistently. Consistency is key. Take the daily objective of parking in a nearby free lot instead of paying to park in the garage closer to your office. You might be annoyed the first few times you make this change. You might have to leave home a little earlier and dress more weather-appropriately. Then, one day you'll walk out with your colleagues, and when they head to the garage and you stroll down the street, the only thing you'll notice is how much money you're saving over time. Your daily action is now a habit.

At different times, you'll find that you need different kinds of inspiration. In this chapter I compile three kinds of success habit tips to keep you on track: Habits to Drive Achievement, Habits to Stay on Track, and Habits of Wealthy People. Any time you get scared, discouraged, or lose your way, look through this chapter to find a habit that just might put you back on the road to success.

Habits to Drive Achievement

Unless you are bestowed an honorary degree, you won't get a Ph.D. in a day or even a year. It happens over time. These habits will help you make sure along the way that you're not getting distracted from whatever it is that your heart desires.

- Have a goal, decide, and commit to it. A clear goal increases your odds of success dramatically. Look back to Chapter 2 if you need help with making SMART goals.

- Get the help you need. You do not have to do it alone. Your dream is your responsibility, but that does not mean you must take on the world alone. You might need a mentor or a helping hand from time to time. The more you ask for help, the easier it gets.

- Do not limit your beliefs. Your goals and excitement propel you forward. Limiting beliefs are like the wind in your face. They will stop you dead in your tracks if you allow them to. Acknowledge the power of negative beliefs that hold you back, and create powerful affirmations for opposing, positive beliefs.

- Visualize your success each day. It is common to focus on the drudgery that lies ahead. That makes it hard to keep your enthusiasm high. Visualizing success maintains your enthusiasm and increases the odds of success. Try closing your eyes during your affirmations and imagine the reality you speak.

- When you're doing goal-oriented activities, find a place as free of distractions as possible. Distractions can take many forms. It might be a noisy neighbor, a messy house, the television, or the internet.

- Expect that you will face a struggle or two. Achieving anything significant will involve at least a couple of setbacks. Your first plan might be misguided. Your second attempt might involve a little bad luck. When obstacles become habits, instead of stressing you out, you'll be confident and motivated to find your way forward.

- Appreciate the process. Big goals can take a lot of time and effort to achieve. If you are not enjoying the process, you are not making the most of your life. If you cannot enjoy the process of achieving your goal, you have the wrong goal.

- Imagine your goal of saving for a second home. It is easy to become too obsessed with your day-to-day finances and be frustrated results aren't instant. Instead, focus on following your savings plan and doing everything you committed to toward this goal. Assume your plan is a good one; your compliance is all that matters. Your compliance drives your results.

Habits to Stay on Track

It's normal to have a setback here and there. Failures and falling short happens to everyone. Successful people take those things in stride and keep going with the habits listed here. Even when things don't go your way, maintaining these habits will help you land on top in the long term.

1. Embrace your failures. The road to success is paved with your failures along the way. Your failures encourage you to try something different or to exert more effort into something. Decide to be okay with failure and to learn from it.

2. Stay focused. Keep working toward your goals one step at a time.

3. Surround yourself with successful people. You are more apt to achieve success if you spend time together with others who are successful.

4. Keep your eyes open for unexpected gems. You might encounter wonderful things that you were not anticipating. Discover the beauty along your path to success. You will then be inspired to continue.

5. Take initiative. Think in advance about what needs to happen for you to surpass a milestone on your journey.

6. Plan. Consistently allow time in your schedule to work toward your desired goals.

7. Use the mini-goals strategy. Rather than setting your goal as, "I want to save $100,000 over the next 10 years," divide up your larger goal for success into segmented goals. In this example, a mini goal could be, "1 will save $10,000 this year" or "1 will save $833 per month each month this year." This way, you will experience frequent successes.

8. Let your creativity flow. Think out of the box.

9. Know your strengths, talents, and skills. Everyone has them. How will they help you achieve success?

10. Utilize the assets you have. Convert your assets into fuel to reach the finish line and achieve success.

11. Take breaks. Occasionally, everyone needs a bit of relaxation to garner the strength to move forward. If you take breaks, you will be bright-eyed, bushy-tailed, and ready to accomplish the success you so truly deserve.

12. Keep a journal collection of your success tips. What works well and what does not.

Habits of Wealthy People

Habits determine the quality of your life. Those who enjoy financial success have money habits that contribute to that success. Add these habits of the wealthy to your life and watch your wealth grow:

1. Review your goals each day. A poll found that 62% of the wealthy have goals and review them daily vs. only 6% of the non-wealthy.

2. Embrace change. Develop the skills and knowledge necessary for growing and evolving.

3. Spend less than you earn. How can your net worth increase if you consistently outspend your income?

4. Avoid spending time on small things. Bigger goals make bigger results.

5. Keep learning. Most financially successful people read daily.

6. Learn to deal with discomfort. We rise to the limit of our ability to deal with discomfort.

7. Delay gratification. Wealthy folks let their money grow.

How many of these habits do you have? More importantly, how many are you willing to add to your life? Remarkable success is the result of good habits followed over an extended period. Apply these suggestions and you will achieve the success you seek. Feel free to add to these lists. Go after your greatest hopes, dreams, and fantasies. It will become habit to attain levels of success that others only dream about.

CHAPTER 5

Creating Systems Toward Success

Now that you understand the power of setting goals and making them a habit, let's put these habits together to make you a manifesto of your dreams. We arrive to our desires, even those big five-year goals, because we follow the path to success. That path is paved with desires and dreams, goals, objectives, habits, and one more thing—*systems*.

A prime example of successful systems is my client, Lana. When we first met, her husband had recently retired from professional golf. She looked at him satisfied with his life's work, and then she looked at herself. Lana had raised the kids, each of whom were great golfers and now had families of their own. And she wanted something of hers. Her idea was to build a nonprofit that teaches golf to underprivileged kids.

"How will you fund it?" I asked.

She blinked at me, confused. Of course, she had done charity work before and knew she needed to fundraise. But she had no idea about the family finances, and there would be upfront costs to create the 501c3. For the first time, she asked her husband about their retirement savings and even his life insurance. What started as one conversation between them became a habit of regular conversations with each financial statement in the mail. They created a budget and found the seed money for her dream. Years later, she has a team of five employees and is developing a golf coaching program to train more volunteer golfers to share the sport through her nonprofit.

Lana got to this five-year dream through setting and achieving many small goals. She and I met each week to discuss her goals, progress, and objectives. And each time our conversations ended with her to-do action steps that I would follow up on in the next session. This became her system to keep her habits, actions, and goals on track and in check.

This is no different from how a successful real estate agent will have a system for generating sales. The system will include getting leads, content marketing, making offers, following up, making sales, and more. There are sales goals, but the system is what moves them toward those weekly, monthly, and yearly sales goals.

Every household has systems, too. You have a system for keeping your lawn tidy. You have a system for making sure you have clean clothes on Monday morning. A system to never run out of cooking oil or yogurt… you get it. You even have a system for brushing your teeth, but it's probably so automatic, you don't think about it.

When you set a new goal, create new systems to support it until it becomes habit. Here's an example of what I mean:

1. Know your goal but focus on how to get there. Imagine that your goal is to go on for a ski vacation in nine months. What if you don't have any current savings and have never skied?

   - With research, you create a budget for how much this family trip will cost, say $10K. You divide that cost across each week as roughly $192. Armed with this knowledge, you can create a plan.

   - Also, look at your fitness. What muscle groups are important for skiing? What movements do you need to be able to do easily? Make your list of what you want to improve, like back and leg strength or balance, to be physically ready for the slopes.

2. Formulate support goals. Break your big goal into several smaller ones that you can isolate and measure to know you're doing the right things to get to your big goal.

   - Each week you need to find $192 to save. Where in your budget are you going to find this money? Good support goals might be not purchasing art or home furnishings, pausing your wine club orders, etc. But don't cancel that gym membership.

   - Your supporting fitness goals will be the number of times per week and length of your work-outs when you'll do weightlifting, cardio, Pilates, etc.

3. Work backward. Create a schedule that starts with what's doable for you in the first week and arrives at your goal in 12 months of paying for your ski trip and being in shape for it.

   - It's unlikely you can go from spending money without a care to total austerity in the blink of an eye. Make a list of spending habits you can commit to now, and each week, add another savings cut. Then another, and another. As you slowly make this transition, you won't feel so deprived and will be more motivated to keep saving when you start to see that ski vacation savings growing.

   - If you're out of shape, don't hit the gym on Day 1 at 100%. Maybe start with one-two days a week with moderate exercises, like light weights, walking, or a recumbent bike. Work up to more days and more vigorous and challenging exercises as your fitness improves (and with a doctor's input, plus maybe a personal trainer if you can do that within your savings plan). Each supporting goal you set will require a different system. Back to real estate, if you have a yearly goal to sell $5 million worth of properties, your systems might be to:

     - Call 25 expired listings each week.

     - Follow up with 25 existing contacts and leads each week.

- Send out 100 postcards each month looking for new buyers and sellers.

- Go to three networking events each month.

Each of these systems have smaller, measurable goals, so while that $5 million sales goal may feel overwhelming, these supporting monthly goals are doable. Follow your system, do the work, and you'll almost be guaranteed to succeed. You could even make more than your yearly goal with the system, and even if you don't hit it exactly, you'll come a lot closer than if you didn't have a solid sales system.

If your system doesn't have measurable supporting goals or is so vague it can't be scheduled, that's a poor system. It will be hard to follow and unlikely to get you to your desired results. Also, if you create a good system but then don't follow it, don't be surprised when you don't achieve your desires. The best system only works for you when you work it.

A sales system that worked well for me was setting aside one hour and calling at least ten prospective clients every weekday, asking how their finances were going, and sharing how my expertise could improve their situation. Lana followed a similar system, but calling prospective donors, sponsors, and volunteers to grow her nonprofit.

CHAPTER 6

There is Power in Giving

I'm sure you've heard of basketball legend, Shaquille O'Neal. But did you know he's also legendary in the charity community? In addition to his Shaquille O'Neal Foundation, he's supported Be the Match, a bone marrow donation organization, the Rainbow PUSH Coalition, supporting technology education for schools with at-risk youth, and Free the Children, which builds schools in developing countries. He's also an Atlanta local and started a Boys and Girls Club here. He's known for visiting our schools, taking pictures with people, and for his random acts of kindness. You just never know what generous, heartfelt thing he's going to do next.

There is power in giving, and you don't have to already be a wealthy celebrity to get involved. Now, I know that household budgets are strained, and giving is more difficult than ever. Everyone is working with reduced resources because of inflation. Most of us feel as though we do not have enough to enjoy our own lives. So, the idea of giving may seem unreasonable. But, if you picked up this book, I suspect you've already been blessed with so much when you look at your life and how rich it really is. Many others are not so fortunate. Consider this:

- 25% of the world's population is starving.
- 15% of the world's population cannot read or write.
- 25 children die every minute from a preventable disease.
- 1.5 billion people do not have access to clean water.

It is not necessary to look far from home to find need. The United States has many homeless people. There are many people not receiving proper nutrition and health care. Some children are not getting the attention they need to flourish. Not to mention the need for better mental health support.

Besides knowing that you helped someone, there are surprising personal benefits to being generous. One of the more profound benefits to the giver is reducing your fear and instilling instead a sense of power. With everything going on in the world, many people live in fear of economic collapse, natural disasters, crime, paying their bills, caring for their children and their parents, and numerous other things. This is a function of real events and the overly sensational coverage by the media. As result, people become more isolated and less connected with society and their community. Many do not even know their neighbors. By giving of your time, you open yourself up to others and your community. And when you contribute to positive changes in whatever way you can, you're being part of the solution to a less scary and more prosperous world.

Plus, reaching your full potential is much more likely when you give. As Mahatma Gandhi says, "To find yourself, lose yourself in the service of others." There was a time when my husband and I were asked to make a big contribution to a cause we believed in. We'd done so in the past, but we were saving our cash to purchase a house. It didn't seem possible to do both, though it weighed on our hearts not to assist the charity. So, we did make the requested donation, thinking this would delay our dream house. However, it didn't. What happened is we got smarter about our budget and more creative with house shopping. We were working toward something bigger than ourselves.

That's why this chapter is about deeply understanding giving so you can set goals to make sure as you rise, you lift others as well. Just like Shaquille.

It is in Your Nature to Give

It is in your nature to give, even if you have forgotten. Think about children: Sure, some of them have an attitude of "mine, mine, and mine," but most are quite giving and share readily. They want to take their friends everywhere with them. They want to feed the baby ducks. They want to take care of their dolls.

However, somewhere along the way, you may have developed the belief that you must keep what you have for yourself. If so, you are punishing yourself by denying your true, giving nature. You are giving into a scarcity mindset of "there's not enough," which will limit your success because you only see a small sliver of what's possible. Instead, you might think, "there's more than enough," so you imagine more and give more without worrying about yourself. If you need more help with this mindset shift, review the positive affirmations teaching in Chapter 1.

So, plan to give what you have. You may have time, money, or both to share with those less fortunate. Give something and witness the impact it has on your life. You'll probably be pleasantly surprised by the power of giving and the benefits it brings into your life. *It is better to give than receive.*

Giving Makes You Wealthy

Review these affirmations on giving that I use in my own life: *I am blessed because I love to bless others. Rather than giving because I am rich; I am rich because I give.* Having money and being rich are two quite different ideas. Many celebrities make millions of dollars and spend every penny without a thought to giving back. They may be rich, but they're not wealthy. The grandness of my wealth cannot be measured by standard measurements. My wealth is of substance and value because it is everlasting.

A large home, an expensive vehicle, and all the luxuries in the world pale in comparison to the feeling I get when I meet a need. Things money can buy are temporary, but the joy of giving lasts a lifetime. Seeing the expression of gratitude and relief in the eyes of a person I have helped is worth more than any possession. By helping others, I become rich in love and relationships.

I give extravagantly, expecting nothing in return. I give to people in need and to people whom I simply want to bless. When I purchase gifts for friends, I give thoughtful gifts of high quality. I become energized about doing something kind for someone else. Before I offer a gift, I am filled with joy and excitement in anticipation of the reaction of the recipient. Seeing the look of joy on someone's face after receiving my gift makes it all worthwhile. My giving comes from the heart; therefore, I continue to give even when I feel empty.

It's important to give freely, with no strings attached. Refrain from competition to give more or better than others, comparing gift sizes, and boasting about your giving. Give based on what you can give, regardless of what others may give. This allows you to give, free from pressure. Whether your gifts are big or small, they expand your wealth.

Giving What You Can

"Commit to the Lord whatever you do, and he will establish your plans." Proverbs 16:3.

Shaquille could just write checks and shut his door, saying he did his part. But he doesn't. He gives of his money, as well as his time, influence, leadership, and friendship. He even gives others the opportunity to join his giving to amplify the positive impact he's making. Even if you don't have a lot of extra cash today, you still have valuable gifts to offer others.

Take an inventory of what you have to give and to whom. Be creative. When I am around my loved ones, I make it a point to be present in the moment and to give all my attention to them. I volunteer my time and financial expertise to worthy causes. You may also have professional skills or talents to donate. What about things like being kind to a checkout clerk who seems to be having a bad day? A musician might offer to play for free at a fundraiser. The possibilities are endless.

Journal about your giving using these prompts to get you started:

1. Why do I give? How does giving enrich my life?

2. What non-material gifts can I share?

3. Whom of my loved ones or others in my community need my gifts?

4. What can I give today?

Look for organizations and ways to give help individually. From local schools and churches to national non-profit organizations, we can all do our part to support the noble work of others.

Here's an affirmation on giving to keep you inspired: *Today, I choose to open my eyes and my wallet to help someone else. I enrich my own life by giving to others.*

Goals for Giving

Refer to your Financial Goals from Chapter 3 to set your financial giving goal. If you're still not sure how to make this commitment, I give you everything you need in Part II to plan your income so you can plan your giving. The second question below invites you to commit to giving of your time, talents, skills, and even your heart.

1. Percent of my income that will go to giving to:

Religious _____   Charites _____   Others _____

Total percentage that will go to donations/giving _____.

2. Nonmaterial Giving Goals:

_____

_____

_____

_____

_____

PART II
FINANCIAL PLANNING

Financial planning is important in numerous ways; it teaches you how to think about money, save and invest a percentage of your income, how to control spending, and manage debt. A target part of financial planning is budgeting well. A budget enables you to make better financial decisions now and in the future by tracking your spending and saving activity. Consistently successful budgeting will lead to financial freedom to enjoy the life of your dreams. The bonus is you can teach what you learned to your loved ones, giving them a head start as they see your living example.

CHAPTER 7

Controlling Spending

A lot of people come to my office and think financial planning is going to be about planning for all that money they will have coming in the future. But while we consider your future earnings, the faster, more direct way for you to keep more cash in your bank account is to control your spending. That doesn't depend on a promotion or bonus, much less winning the lottery. You can grow the money you have simply by leaving more of it in your pocket.

Let's start by seeing how well you control your spending now. Read the personal financial narrative below and notice which parts you do or don't identify with today:

I pave the road to financial security by controlling my spending. In times when most families are struggling to make ends meet, I consider myself fortunate to have financial security. By controlling my spending habits, I minimize our bills and even make a considerable contribution to our savings account every few weeks.

I can remember a time when I found myself living paycheck to paycheck. I had to worry about how I would scramble together the money to pay my electric bill, buy gas for my car, pay my rent, mortgage, or buy food.

Now, however, I am free from that sense of panic and financial instability. Recalling the tough times helps me put the brakes on my spending and build up my savings account.

Do I need HBO and Showtime in my cable package? No.

Do I need my Grande Caramel Macchiato from Starbucks each morning? No.

Packing my lunch saves me $5 to $10 each day or up to $100 to $200 each month.

By removing these inexpensive splurges from my budget, I can save $2,400 to $3,600 per year. That money serves a better purpose of earning interest in my high-yield savings account. Today, I continue to curb my spending by focusing on the result, knowing that a small sacrifice now leads to big financial security later. For example, a sizable savings and emergency fund. Rather than depriving myself, I am simply forgoing a few luxuries in exchange for a better tomorrow.

When I want to buy 'just one little purse" or "just one pair of tennis shoes," I dissuade myself by envisioning my savings account hitting five digits. *Oh, how sweet it is.*

Did you have more in common with what the speaker's life used to be like or how it is today? Which way of spending and saving sounds more like you? Be honest with yourself.

Answer these journal prompts to reflect on your spending:

1. How can I minimize my daily, weekly, and monthly expenses?
2. What luxuries can I eliminate from my routine?
3. How much money can I comfortably transfer into my savings account each month?

Fortunately, whatever situation you're in now, from uncontrolled spending to just barely missing your savings targets, you'll find support and insight in the coming chapters of Part II.

CHAPTER 8

Why Budgeting Matters

Wouldn't it be great to have enough money to live your life to its fullest while still putting away plenty for a rainy day? You can turn this dream into a reality if you are willing to plan and stick to a budget. A well-planned budget enables you to make financial decisions that support your happiness and peace of mind. With a budget, you see exactly where each dollar you earn is being spent. This helps you spend less on items that don't fit your life's priorities. As a result, you have more money to spend on things that matter to you.

This chapter builds on what you just learned about controlling your spending. You've already brainstormed some obvious changes you can make to spend less on things you don't actually *need*. Budgeting takes that a step further by helping you plan for the spending you have to do for bills and necessities, as well as putting money into savings for specific goals—and to plan not to do "extra" spending. When you know where all your money is going, you're empowered to make wise financial choices.

If you think staying on a budget is difficult, you may be pleasantly surprised because many of my clients find it easier than they thought when they follow plans we create together—like Bob and Susan that you met in Chapter 1. Their budget allowed them to stay in their house even while making career changes and accepting salary cuts, not to mention that they paid off their credit card debts and started saving. When you plan your budget carefully, you create the right mix of spending and saving to support you in the pursuit of your dreams.

How to Plan Your Budget for Financial Solvency

Contrary to widespread belief, planning a budget allows you to experience more of the fun things in life. Many believe that sticking to a budget robs them of life's adventure and spontaneity. A well-crafted budget, however, ensures that funds are available for instant adventures as well as planned expenses.

The first step in creating your budget is to gather the things you will need. Among them are your bank statements, bills, and information about how much cash you have available. It's also helpful to know how much you're spending on necessities like food and gasoline.

The budget you create can be as simple as a handwritten document or a small spreadsheet on your computer. The important thing is that the budget helps you to track what you spend and keep your financial life organized.

To plan your budget, consider these questions:

- How much money do you have right now?
- What are you spending your money on?
- Where can you cut back?
- What will you gain by spending less?
- What do you want to save for?
- What are your plans for the future?

When you know what you want and where you are going financially, you can create a plan to help you get there. *Do not be afraid to dream big and make room in your budget for joy.*

Using a Budget to Meet Goals

With a budget, you are more likely to achieve your financial goals. Just like any life goals, break your money goal down into a series of smaller goals to keep from getting overwhelmed. At a high level, this is about tracking your spending, committing to a plan that supports your financial goals, and remaining flexible. The sense of accomplishment as you achieve these small goals will keep you moving forward—especially when you have a significant other and work together on your budget.

Remember that it is okay to adjust your budget; it's a flexible roadmap, not written in stone. Our first budget may need tweaks, but that budget is the first step to the financial freedom and peace of mind you deserve. You don't have to do everything perfectly from the beginning, but you do have to pick somewhere and start following your saving, spending, and saying, 'no" plan. Getting your finances under control can lead to more monetary security in the future. Stay organized with tracking your actual spending against your budget's forecast and adjust your budget as you go.

Plan your budget with your significant other if you have one. Ensure that the budget you create supports things that are important to both of you so you'll both be motivated to make the short-term sacrifices necessary for your long-term financial freedom. Setting a budget should be a joint effort so you both make arguments for things you don't want to lose and offer changes you're willing to commit to. When you both have buy-in, you're more likely to hold each other accountable and even strengthen your relationship as you strengthen your finances.

Four Steps to a Solid Budget

Your budget brings your mind, family, and finances into harmony, dramatically reducing money stress. The challenges of life become much more manageable when you know you can pay for everything you need, have savings for surprise expenses, and are working toward big financial goals. This is how a budget allows you to take control of your finances, instead of your finances controlling you. They key is to create a budget that supports your dreams, while making sure the necessities are taken care of. The Four Steps to a Solid Budget will guide you:

1. Find the starting line. The first crucial step in creating a household budget that works is to list all your income and keep track of every dime you spend for a month. Before you can know where you are going, you must know your starting point. You'll be surprised to learn where your money goes each month. Awareness alone may change your spending habits for the better.

2. Use credit wisely and sparingly. In college, using credit cards can seem like no big deal. Credit card issuers often give exclusive deals and incentives to lure college students into applying for credit they do not need. With large spending limits and small incomes, credit cards tempt you to live a lifestyle you cannot afford.

Credit, used properly, can provide convenience and peace of mind in knowing that you are covered in the case of an emergency. But the temptation is great to live outside of your means and worry about paying for those purchases later. The fewer credit cards you sign up for, the less you will be tempted to spend away from your future financial health.

3. Keep your checkbook balanced. One of the simplest and most productive habits you can incorporate into your financial success plan is to maintain a balanced checkbook. Keep track of everything that goes in and out of your account by writing it in your check register or a spreadsheet. At the end of the month, compare your checkbook to your bank statement.

When you are keeping track of what you spend, you may feel less tempted to waste money on impulse purchases. You will also always know when the money is almost out. This can save you a lot of money on overdraft fees and a lot of headaches.

4. Reduce expenses. There is no secret to a successful budget. It's as simple as keeping track of your income and expenses, increasing your income, or lowering your expenses until you spend less than you earn, while also saving for a rainy day.

Once you have a good grasp on what you are spending and where to find places to cut back, put the money you save into a savings account for a rainy day. Clip coupons, look for sales, including grocery sales. Turn off the lights when you leave the room, turn the air conditioner off when you leave the house, and cook ahead of time to save on the expense of eating out.

Financial pressures can make all of life seem overwhelming at times. If you implement these simple steps and commit to maintaining a rock-solid budget for your family, you will experience financial peace and prosperity. Beyond that, however, every area of your life will improve, as you will be more relaxed and at ease with the peace of mind you've achieved.

To create your budget, use the worksheets in the back of the book. Also, review the Budgeting Action Steps Tips Sheet on the following pages.

CHAPTER 9

Getting Yourself Out of Debt

Let's talk about good debt, which is typically associated with low-interest rates, tax advantages, and long-term financial benefits. For example, if you receive a home improvement loan to remodel your home. You later sell it, and you recover the cost of the repairs at closing, this is considered good debt.

Bad debt refers to borrowing money for items or expenses that do not hold or generate long-term value. Examples of bad debt include credit card debt: Accumulating credit card debt for non-essential purchases or expenses can be considered bad debt due to high-interest rates and potential financial strain. Payday loans: These short-term, high-interest loans often come with excessive fees and can lead to a cycle of debt. Consumer loans for depreciating assets: taking out loans for items that quickly lose value, such as electronics or vehicles, can be viewed as bad debt.

Often, as my clients create their budgets, they're surprised how much debt they have. It's very understandable that with it being so easy to apply for a credit card and almost every store offering some kind of credit or payment plans, people often have more debt than just college tuition, car payments, or mortgage payments. All this debt adds up, and if you're just making the minimum payments, it may feel that your debts are insurmountable.

The good news is that no matter how high the mountain appears, you can climb it and pull yourself out of the metaphorical hole you may find yourself in.

Here are some ways to tackle that debt and bring it down to size:

1. Only buy what you can afford. The best way to keep debt from becoming a problem is to avoid the problem altogether from this point forward. Rather than splurging on a fancy piece of electronic hardware by using credit, just wait and save for it

By staying within budget and paying off your bills every month, you do not need to worry about debt piling up on top of you.

- You can get out of debt and feel the sweet relief of being debt-free by changing your mindset from "having it now" to one of enjoying it even more when you have the money.

2. Pay off the lowest balance first. Financial advisor, Suze Orman often advises people in debt to take care of the higher interest debts first. In general, this is an effective way to go; however, if you have a credit card with a balance of only a couple hundred dollars, it would also be beneficial to knock that one off right out of the gate.

- You can eliminate a whole payment, save on interest charges, and put that money toward another bill.

3. Prioritize bills by interest rate. Overall, paying off the higher interest cards first will save you the most money. It's usually the interest that keeps knocking you back, by taking out the higher interest cards you'll feel a greater sense of progress when paying your bills every month.

4. Consolidate. One of the more overwhelming aspects of being in credit card debt is constantly being reminded of it with so many bills from different cards. One way to fight back is to consolidate your debt. You can do this by either taking out a loan from a bank or transferring the balance to another card.

- If you recently got a new credit card, you could transfer a portion of the balance to that. This will save you a bit of interest since most cards will put that balance under the introductory rate.

- If you take out a loan, you can pay off several of the cards and reduce the amount of mail you receive. It is less daunting psychologically to receive one big bill as opposed to a bunch of tiny ones.

5. Convert to cash and debit only. One of the best ways to keep yourself in debt is to keep using your credit cards. They are convenient and it's easy to justify their occasional use by saying that it's only a soda or a tank of gas, but those purchases come with a hefty fee in interest rates and keep you in the cycle of debt.

- Those tiny charges add up quickly! A dollar here, a few more there, and you will negate the payments that you're making in a very short amount of time.

- Paying with cash will help you develop new spending habits. By the time you get your debts paid down, you will have disciplined yourself to the point where you no longer put yourself in that situation.

Debt is a problem that happens to everyone at some point. Even wealthy people find themselves overextended and carrying debt. Even if you are working on a shoestring budget, it is possible to pull yourself out of debt. With discipline, focus, and arduous work, you can find yourself relieved of the mounting pressures.

Let's look at the true cost of a car which can be calculated by adding the purchase price of the car to the total interest paid. It's important to compare different loan offers, negotiate favorable terms, and consider the impact of interest rates and loan terms on the overall cost.

For example, if you purchase a car for $25,000 with a 5-year loan term and an interest rate of 4%, the total cost of the car would include the interest paid over the loan term. Assuming no down payment, the total interest paid would be $2,304, resulting in a total cost of $27,304.

The best reason to pay off debt is to save money and avoid paying interest. Also, it makes you feel great not owing anyone. The scores are the industry standard for making accurate lending practices. Millions of people have received good credit ratings and have purchased homes, cars, boats, and more.

FICO Score

Your FICO (Fair Isaac Corporation) credit score measures your consumer credit risk. The score is used by many lenders and often ranges from 300-850. A FICO Score above 670 or so is considered a good score. You may order a free FICO score from myFICO.com and credit reports from all three bureaus: Experian, TransUnion, and Equifax.

Knowing you credit score helps you apply for loans like a mortgage, auto loan or credit card, with confidence. When you apply for credit, lenders may use one or more of these bureaus. It is also, a great practice to review you reports at least once a year for errors. Fixing errors in your credit report may have a significant impact on your credit score. I am aware of several clients whom discovered errors on their reports and immediate disputed the errors and their reports are now accurate. Always, monitor your reports.

Credit scores directly affect mortgage rates and a difference of 100 points could cost or save you thousands. Without a high credit score, you will not qualify for the best mortgage rates available, which could mean you will end up paying more money over the term of you mortgage. For example, the difference between 3% and 3.25% can add up over a 30-year fixed-rate mortgage.

Estate Planning

Estate planning determines how your assets are distributed align with your preferences. It provides you with control over your assets, protects your loved ones, and helps you leave a legacy. It is a proactive approach that ensures your wishes are honored and minimized potential legal and financial complications for your beneficiaries, Consulting with an estate planning attorney or financial advisor can help you create a comprehensive plan tailored to your specific needs and goals.

Estate planning can help minimize the tax burden on your estate and maximize the assets that are passed on to your beneficiaries. Various estate planning tools and strategies, such as trusts and gifting, can be utilized to reduce estate taxes or avoid them altogether.

For parents with minor children, estate planning is essential to appoint guardians who will care for and raise their children in the event of their premature death. It allows you to specify who will assume the responsibility of providing for and making decisions regarding your children's upbringing.

Estate planning can help minimize potential conflicts and disputes among family members regarding the distribution of assets. Clearly outlining your wishes in a legally binding manner can prevent disagreements and provide clarity and peace of mind to your loved ones.

Estate planning included documents like a power of attorney and healthcare directives designate individuals to make financial and medical decisions on your behalf if you become incapacitated. It allows you to choose trusted individuals who will handle your affairs and make decisions according to your wishes.

Business succession planning- If you own a business, estate planning is essential for a smooth transition and continuity of the business upon your retirement, incapacitation, or death. It allows you to plan for the transfer of ownership, address potential tax implications, and ensure the ongoing success of the business.

Life Insurance

Life insurance is an essential part of financial planning. One reason most people buy life insurance is to replace income that would be lost with the death of a bread winner. The cash provided by life insurance also can help ensure that your dependents are not burdened with significate debt when you die. Life insurance proceeds could mean your dependents will not have to sell assets to pay outstanding bills or taxes. An important feature of life insurance is that no income tax is payable on proceeds paid to beneficiaries.

A common question asked, when buying life insurance is how much is needed. First, you should assemble personal financial information and review your family's needs. There are severa factors to consider when determining how much protection you should have. These include:

- Any immediate needs at the time of death, such as final illness expenses, burial costs, and estate taxes

- Funds for a readjustment period, to finance a move, or to provide time for family members to find a job.

- Ongoing financial needs, such as monthly bills and expenses, day-care costs, college, tuition, or retirement

- Business continuity of a self-employed owner

Although there is no substitute for carefully evaluating the coverage needed to meet your needs, one rule of thumb used is, to buy life insurance that is equal to five to seven times your annual gross income.

A family member had lung cancer that quickly metastasized to her brain, and she passed away. within seven weeks. She knew I did estate planning, but she didn't have a will or life insurance because she didn't want to think about dying. She only had less than $1,000 cash, so other family members had to make all the choices and expenses for her funeral and interment. In short, have enough life insurance to cover your funeral expenses.

Long Term Care

Long Term Care is the assistance individuals need when they are unable to care for themselves and need help with Activities of Daily Living (ADLs) – bathing, dressing, transferring, toileting, continence (control of bodily functions), and eating – or they have severe cognitive impairments such an Alzheimer's disease. Long-term care needs can result from an accident, chronic illness or short-term disability, or advanced age.

During scheduled meetings, we discuss Long-term Care, and the younger clients brush off the need to consider this coverage and resolve to wait until they are older. Just like life insurance, the older you become the more the insurance premiums will cost.

The following are major types of Long-Term Care and the kinds of services you may need. The plans and coverages are not discussed in great details but rather you are referred to the Eldercare Locator.

- Home Care, Community Services, Supportive Housing Programs, Assisted Living, Continuing Care Retirement Communities (CCRCs), Nursing Homes, and Intermediate Care Facilities for the Mentally Retarded.

You can learn about long term care options in your area by contacting the Eldercare Locator at

1-800-677-1116.

Budgeting Action Steps Tips

1. Set financial goals.

2. Create a spending plan.

3. Avoid credit card debt.

4. Save at least 10% of your gross pay.

5. Create an emergency fund.

6. Seek professional advice from an estate planning attorney.

7. Seek advice from a finance expert.

PART III
ABUNDANCE AND MINDSET

Everyone talks about abundance in Churches, Universities, Corporations, the Government, social media, and in your homes. Abundance means different things to different people. It is important to identify what it means to you and how it enables you to live your best life. Abundance is money, attitude, good relationships, mindset, health, fitness, being spiritually fortified, and appreciating what you already have. Whatever the meaning of abundance is to you, you want to manage your assets well to enjoy the benefits.

A positive or negative attitude is vital because it affects your income proportionately to your mindset. Having a positive viewpoint is an asset that can attract financial opportunities to assist you in reaching your goals. Therefore, take the steps down the right path with a winning attitude that will attract what you want in life, currently and later into retirement.

CHAPTER 10

What is Abundance About?

Abundance is about more than money, being rich, or even wealth. Some people equate financial success with abundance. Yes, having enough money is a significant part of abundance, but there's much more to it. You can be wealthy and be alone. You can have money and be in poor health. You can be financially successful and be miserable. You can be the wealthiest person in the world and still not experience abundance.

My client, Colette, learned this the hard way. Before working with me, she built a profitable string of successful candle stores. She'd started out with one small retail shop, ringing up the sales herself. Over time she hired staff, even a marketing team, and she took herself out of the day-to-day operations. That sounds like an entrepreneur's dream, right?

It was, until the dividend checks every month started to feel easy. She fell into a friendship with an independently wealthy woman who had money from two divorces. There's nothing wrong with having money that way, but this woman didn't value it. She encouraged Colette to spend extravagantly and not to worry so much about planning for the future—she certainly didn't. When it came to other people's struggles, Colette had been generous before, sharing her expertise and financial donations. But this new friend convinced her if someone didn't have money or necessities, it was their fault. Not Colette's.

She said, "I was as cold-hearted as Marie Antoinette when she said, 'Let them eat cake.' Now I'm the one struggling."

You see, the friend had convinced her that marketing expenses were a waste and that she didn't need to keep expanding her locations. The business stagnated, and when it was in trouble, Colette didn't have the cash to bail herself out. She had to file for bankruptcy and closed her candle stores. By the time she visited me, she felt like a failure and was convinced her previous success was luck, and that now she needed to protect what little assets she had left. Oh, and the divorcee friend stopped returning Colette's calls.

I listened to her story, mostly quietly and taking notes. When she finished, I told her, "I don't think you have a money problem. It sounds like you have an abundance mindset problem."

She furrowed her brows at me. "This isn't in my head. It's in my bank account," she said.

Still, she trusted me to help her. We started with goal setting, tracking her progress, achieving goals, and protecting her assets. Before she could be successful again, she had to believe it and then take action on belief to move closer to her goals every day. Without belief in herself and her ability to attract money and wealth, she was half-heartedly going through the motions with little to show for it. We increased her belief in herself with positive affirmations that reframe the negative thoughts and beliefs Colette learned from her friend.

Currently, she's saving, reinvesting, and rebuilding her business. She remembers again how she planned and sacrificed to achieve her wealth the first time—and now she's doing it again. Colette is living an abundant lifestyle, positively influencing those around her and being a good steward of her blessings. And rebuilding her finances started with her believing it was possible.

Nine Abundance Beliefs

Abundance is a mindset and a belief system. It is a way of viewing the world, the people in it, and yourself. It is deciding to believe that the universe will provide if you hold up your end of the bargain.

Want to know if you have an abundance mindset? Consider which of these nine abundance beliefs you hold:

1. Abundance is an attitude. Money is money, but abundance is a mindset. It is a decision to believe that you can have whatever you need, in the quantities you need it. It is the belief that there is always enough.

2. Abundance is having an excess of important resources. True abundance is not just money. It is also about having enough of the other necessary resources in your life. This can include things like free time, love, and happiness. Money is important, but there is much more to abundance than money.

3. Abundance is the belief that there is enough for everyone. Those obsessed with wealth are often competitive and believe that there is only a finite amount of wealth to be divided among everyone. Abundance is the belief that there is enough for everyone.

4. Abundance has a greater impact on happiness than wealth. Abundance increases the likelihood of happiness. Great wealth is no more likely to make you happy than a decent middle-class income. There's research to support this idea. You cannot make yourself happier by accumulating great wealth.

5. Abundance avoids attachment. Abundance lacks attachment. There is no reason to hold on tightly to what you have if you believe there will always be enough in the future. With an abundance mindset, you feel comfortable allowing everything to flow into and out of your life.

6. Abundance allows you to dream bigger. Abundance allows for the biggest of dreams to

become a possibility in your mind. Money provides opportunities, but only for those things, you can afford. Abundance takes the possibilities in your life to another level.

7. Abundance avoids resentment. With abundance, there is no reason to be jealous or resentful of someone else's success. The success of one person cannot negatively impact the success of someone else.

8. Those with an abundant mindset are grateful. Gratitude is part of abundance. You can't experience abundance unless you're grateful for what you have. Gratitude creates the possibility of receiving even more in the future. How grateful are you right now?

9. Abundance leads to positive expectations. When you believe in abundance, you are positive about the future. You expect good things to happen and to continue happening.

How much abundance do you have in your life? How would you measure abundance?

What does abundance mean to you? You cannot acquire what you don't identify.

Resist the urge to believe that all your challenges will be solved with money. Once your money issues are solved, you have a whole new set of problems to deal with. You just could not see them before.

For example, you do not care too much about your unreliable car if you are in the process of drowning in the lake. You do not see your loneliness as a problem if you are struggling to buy food each month. Money solves certain challenges, but more challenges are waiting for you.

Abundance can solve far more challenges than money. Seek abundance in all forms. This is much more powerful than just a large bank account.

An abundant life is a mindset; you must see or visualize your abundant life before living it. Once one goal is reached, and you celebrate the great feeling you get, work on the next goal. Work on this goal daily, and you will have it based on your commitment to it and what you measure. I have witnessed many great success stories besides Colette's. Let's add yours to the list.

CHAPTER 11

Living an Abundant Life

As much as abundance starts with belief, as you learned in the last chapter, it's also a lifestyle. Living an abundant life includes all aspects of life, for instance, financial, spiritual, family, health, career/ business, leisure, and education. Life has its way of testing your abilities to find out where you are weak and strong. Sometimes we're all tested, as in natural disasters or global events with wide impacts, and other times we're tested individually. If you've ever felt like success is easier for those around you than for yourself, this was likely such a test. When you fail the test, you go into reverse where life tries to teach that principle again. This can hurt and be uncomfortable when you lose momentum or suffer a setback.

When this occurs, collect yourself and fight for your abundant life by remembering your goals, purpose, and the reasons you desire this life. Develop a written plan with goals and action steps you've learned in this book to help you get back on track. A divorce or loss of a loved one is a common life challenge. As emotional as these are, you must analyze the circumstances, set aside time to heal, and plan your attack for recovery. Review your budget and expenses to adjust if necessary. If you need to replace lost income, develop a means to generate more. If it's loneliness, socialize with friends, date, meet new people, and be active. The abundance lost can be rebuilt if you believe it's yours and are willing to work for it.

Build Your Abundant Life

A life filled with physical, emotional, spiritual, and financial abundance is truly a gift. Everyone should have security, peace of mind, love, and overall joyfulness. But how can something that should be second nature be so difficult to attain? Perhaps our hectic lives confuse or distract us from achieving a life of abundance. Sometimes, as with Colette, we forget our abundance beliefs and are influenced by others. But the power of our thoughts can transform our lives for the better if we harness it.

Do you believe this statement? *Wealth is Good.* If so, you may have the makings of an abundant lifestyle. If not, why not? It's possible you're thinking of wealth like having millions of dollars and flying a private jet to one of your five estate homes. That can be wealth, but wealth can simply mean having a steady, full-time job where you earn enough money to give your family a safe place to sleep with quality food on the table and nice clothes to wear. It may also mean you are fulfilled spiritually and emotionally.

We all have to build wealth in our lives to support ourselves and our families. Oh, and don't fool yourself by saying you do not care about material things and, therefore, you don't need to care too much about building wealth. Remember that wealth does not necessarily mean material wealth. Just because you desire wealth, it does not mean you have to be attached to money like a Scrooge.

You can be emotionally wealthy because of the positive relationships you foster. You can be spiritually wealthy because of your faith. You can be physically wealthy because of your vibrant health. And you can be financially wealthy because of the money you have earned.

Wealth is Not Just About Money

As mentioned, the term wealth does not just describe how much money you have. You can also use the word to describe the people in your life and your satisfaction with your life in general.

- If you have a close relationship with your family, you are wealthy.

- If you love waking up in the morning and getting satisfaction out of your job every day, you are wealthy.

- If you have friends who love you like their own family, you are wealthy,

- If you have a fervent faith, you are wealthy.

Living an abundant life simply means being happy in all aspects of your life and having the resources to care for your family. Obviously, you won't be happy every minute of every day, but if you are usually well taken care of, then you already have an abundant life.

Abundance is about taking care of others—and yourself. This is harder for nurturing people who were taught to put others first. That's a wonderful quality, and you also must nurture yourself. Loving yourself is of great importance to attract love and positivity in return. You must love yourself first if you want to receive love from others, right? If you don't have love from others, you won't lead the life you desire. We know this applies to relationships, but it also applies to wealth. How can we expect life to treat us richly when we treat ourselves poorly?

Next time you eat out and set a budget for yourself when everything on the menu costs more, do you eat soup and suffer? That is a poverty mindset. Or, you can have a wealthy mindset and set your expectations to enjoy yourself and a pleasant meal in a lovely environment. Being confident that you can support yourself and deserve a nice meal (obviously if you aren't putting it on a credit card).

You need to carry a positive mindset in life if you wish to build the wealth you want and deserve. You must believe that what you want can be attained, that you have the power to attain it, and that it will be delivered to you in your lifetime. Without this mindset, you're more likely to give up when times get tough.

We can't change the world unless we start by changing ourselves. But if we change ourselves, we can change the whole world. And if we change ourselves for the better, there's no reason why we cannot or should not live an abundant life.

CHAPTER 12

Manifesting Wealth and Abundance

In Chapter 1 I told you there three things to do to achieve success: Define it, take action, and *manifest*. The first two are easy to understand, but this third one. What I don't mean is trying to 'manifest' by just making vision board and wishing your dreams would just magically come true. However, manifesting wealth and abundance begins from within. You must appreciate what you have in your life already — your family, friends, and job — instead of focusing on what you wish you had.

Often people waste precious time thinking about what they do not have. They start to believe their lives will improve if only they had more money, more friends, or more gadgets. They think about what's lacking instead of the abundance that is already overflowing into their life. *Negative thoughts bring more lack.*

I once knew a man, Richard, who completed an MBA with a mission to do a particular job at one company and wouldn't take advantage of opportunities that didn't fit this rigid profile. There needed to be a job good enough for him; in other words, he would decline the position and remain unemployed if the job did not pay a specific amount. He was unemployed for some time due to his pickiness and had to adhere to a tight budget as his savings ran out. Time ticked by, and he started lashing out at others for no reason and thinking the worst of anyone who tried to offer a suggestion. He lost his home, many friends, good health, and career opportunities. As the adage goes, you become what you think about. All he thought about was what he didn't have, and finally he didn't have much. This was a sad case.

However, *positive thoughts bring more abundance.* Positive thinking produces positive action—just the opposite situation of a person with a negative mindset. With a positive mindset, Richard would've negotiated better salaries and terms for any attractive position. He might not have stayed in an entry position long, but his career options would've kept improving, and he would've kept researching greater opportunities. Keeping your goal front and center and reciting your abundance is powerful. Richard could've taken progressively higher-paying jobs until he landed the one, he desired, lived within his budget, and, importantly, kept a positive attitude.

It takes self-confidence, desire, determination, positive recitations, and a measurable plan of action to manifest wealth and abundance. With this in place, there is little or no room for failure. If you appreciate what you have, you will be inspired to take the necessary actions to bring more of what you want into your life. From a practical point of view, this all starts with living happily with what you have.

Now, this may sound counterproductive at first, but living happily with what you have doesn't mean you're completely satisfied and fulfilled. It simply means that you appreciate all the good parts of your life and recognize that you can take those things you have, even if they are few, and build upon them. Very often we take our lives for granted and forget to give thanks for all that is good. If you're having a tough time recognizing the goodness in your life, make a gratitude list and continue adding to it daily.

For example:

- Be thankful when paying the rent because this means you have a place to sleep.

- Be thankful for your winter coat because you'll stay warm this winter.

- Be thankful for your family because of their love, support, and guidance.

- Be thankful for your job because it has allowed you to support your family.

If you can be happy with what you have now, you'll have a deeper appreciation for the better circumstances that are coming to you in your future. Just imagine how much more you'll appreciate your eventual move to a large home with a spacious property when you begin to enjoy your current humble place.

Remember, the term "wealth" doesn't only relate to money. You can be wealthy by having a loving family who visits often or friends who care for you like one of their own. There's much more to life than who has the latest designer purse or fanciest sports car in the neighborhood.

First Steps Toward Wealth

When you do not have a lot of material possessions and monetary wealth, it ironically becomes easier for you to learn how to save money. Saving money is paramount if you want to build monetary wealth, but to do so, you must learn how to delay gratification. That means you must make sure you are making more money than you are spending. Ideally, you want to pay for everything you have, not finance it— without truly owning your possessions and going into debt, you are moving farther away from wealth.

Besides saving money, the tangible way to build wealth is to make more money. Too many people are not making the money they can and should. You must consciously decide to get unstuck from your dead-end job and the rat race.

You must rise above the crowd and do something different. That may mean you have to discover creative ways for you to make more money. For many people today, that may mean getting involved in a virtual office or an Internet-based business, but whatever the case might be for you, you can elevate yourself.

If you are unhappy with the money you are making, you must start thinking about ways to increase the amount of money you make so you can realize your dreams.

CHAPTER 13

Think Like the Top 1%

It is imperative to think and grow rich, as Napoleon Hill says. This philosophy has been tried and tested as thousands have become rich because of this thinking. His point is that we have a desire, plan, positive mindset, persistence, and focus to achieve our wildest dreams. If you desire abundance, you must choose to think differently.

For instance, a real estate broker, Ruth, acquired a 50-property portfolio—while working in two careers. She worked diligently as an insurance broker and real estate agent to build a successful real estate empire. I remember our discussions that the larger source of income was coming from real estate. This did not deter her from working in both fields, which was her goal. With persistent actions, this plan paid great dividends—an investing system led to wealth.

She intended to have two sources of income, so she always had two levers to pull in case one sector slowed down. The top 1% of the wealthiest people in the world have multiple streams of income so they don't rely on any one paycheck for everything. She had the mindset that she didn't have to put 100% of her energy into any one field. With this mindset of multiple income streams with efficient systems in place, she achieved her goals automatically.

The top 1% of billionaires and multi-millionaires is not just working harder than the bottom 99%. You must find your way to the top. Prominent levels of success do require demanding work, but the work must be smart, too. The bottom 99% focus on the wrong things, prioritize short-term comfort over success, and fail to take enough action. The top 1% are not smarter or more capable, but they use their time wisely and manage themselves effectively.

Here are ten differences between the top 1% and everyone else:

1. Being the only one is better than being the best. One famous quote goes, competition is for losers. While the average person that wants to aspire to great accomplishments is concerned with being the best, the ultra-successful look for ways to avoid competition. Create a new market or field. Be the only one.

2. They attack the day early. They get a good start on the day. While the other 99% are trying to figure out what to do, the top 1% are already busy. They have enthusiasm in the morning and make the most of the early hours.

3. Action trumps knowledge. The top 1% are knowledgeable, but they know a secret. A good plan that is followed aggressively and persistently always beats a great plan that is implemented half-heartedly. Know what you need to know and then get busy making it happen. An unquenchable thirst for knowledge is often fear in disguise.

4. Goals are achieved by systems. A system of eating nutritiously and exercising results in health and fitness. A system of saving and investing leads to wealth. The top 1 % look for effective systems to implement. With the right systems in place. goals are attained automatically.

5. They have priorities. Having too many priorities results in having none. You cannot be a world-class artist, dog trainer, yoga expert, and bowler. Be strong enough to whittle down your priorities to the few that matter most to you. Having too many priorities is a path to mediocrity.

6. The top 1% make networking a priority. You can never have too many friends. Anyone can learn good networking skills. Having many long-term acquaintances can be powerful. You will have a constant supply of assistance and opportunities. Knowing the right people is an important part of becoming part of the top 1%..

7. They make money a priority, and are not simply good at saving. They are also good at investing their money wisely. They pay their bills on time, avoid unnecessary debt, and get professional help when necessary. Manage your money wisely and join them.

8. They are aware of their weaknesses. The top 1% know what they can and cannot do. They avoid their weaknesses or find a way to deal with them. Play to your strengths.

9. They focus on the long term. Delaying gratification is a key to becoming extraordinarily successful. Let the average people satisfy their short-term cravings. Keep your eye on the grand prize.

10. They emphasize finding solutions to their challenges. The key to making a lot of money or achieving challenging goals is in resolving your challenges. Search for solutions and stay focused on the issue itself. Find a solution and get to work.

Anyone can become part of the top 1%, but it requires a change in thinking and focus. Set your priorities and stick to them. Manage your money wisely and network like your life depends on it. Focus on developing the right systems to achieve your goals and emphasize action. Only action will bring the results you desire. You will find networking rewarding and profitable, I promise you.

CHAPTER 14

Boost Your Income by Boosting Your Attitude

Remember in Chapter 6 when I shared about when my husband and I made a significant charitable donation while saving for a new home? Well, the changes we made weren't just about budgeting. We also had to improve our attitudes toward the situation. At first, I cried, imagining donating that money. This donation required a spiritual sacrifice, too. We donated, believed, prayed, and asked God to bless and honor us with our desired dream home. As a result of this donation, which was the largest we'd ever made, we also believed our income would increase.

That's because we made this donation in the spirit of an abundance mindset. We knew a wealthier lifestyle was on the horizon. We would associate with people of more influence through this donation, enriching our lives. And in the end, our dreams materialized. We became the people we needed to be and did the work we needed to do to accomplish our goals. This was about working hard and learning, as well as thinking positively. Vast opportunities are available to everyone who believes and takes action on those beliefs.

We often allow our actions to be ruled by our emotions, like fear. It's a fact: negative thoughts and feelings harm every aspect of our lives, from family to work and social lives.

What would things be like if we transformed negative thoughts into positive ones? Changing how we feel about ourselves can change our direction in life! Living in the present and having a positive outlook on our future can help us reach goals we once thought was impossible. A brighter outlook on life can open our eyes to more possibilities and encourage us to move in new and exciting directions.

How can you attain a better outlook on life? It all has to do with the way you see yourself. Having a positive and outgoing attitude is the key to changing your self-concept, boosting your income, and improving your life.

Here are some techniques you can use to boost your attitude:

1. Get control. Figure out the things that make you unhappy and find ways to change them for the better. A positive outlook can change everything in your life—you just need to believe in yourself first.

- Loving yourself is the only way you're going to allow others to see you in a positive light as well. If you project negativity, you'll be viewed as a negative person.

- Realizing you can't control how others think and feel about you is critical to getting control of yourself.

- You have the power to work on ways to make yourself happy. Avoid doing something for the sole purpose of making someone else happy. It must be about you. This isn't about being selfish; it's about being true to you.

2. Change the way you think. Negative thoughts beget negative actions. Make a conscious effort to change the way you react and deal with situations. Look for the silver lining instead of focusing on the negative attributes of situations and people.

- If you think positively, you'll act positively. Those positive thoughts and actions will keep many anxieties at bay. Through positive thoughts and actions, anything can become a reality.

3. Be your cheerleader. You're your own best cheering section. So many times, in life, the things we do go unrecognized by others, whether it's at home or work. When this happens, step in and praise yourself.

- Private affirmations can make you feel better about yourself when others fail to verbalize their gratitude.

- By actively projecting a positive outlook of yourself, you will push yourself further to do better the next time. Doing so will also bring you the confidence to explore more areas in life.

4. Dream it into reality. Misery loves company, and if you believe you'll never achieve anything, you can create a self-fulfilling prophecy. Dream big and dream often!

- Figure out what you want in life and set your dreams into motion. Want a better job? Take the necessary steps to make it happen. You're the biggest obstacle holding you back.

A positive attitude can change your job situation, relationships, and life. If you feel better about yourself, other people will feel the good vibrations you're giving off. You'll appear more confident and have a better chance of taking on whatever life throws at you.

If you believe in yourself, you can continue to accomplish bigger and better things. Whether you're working to advance yourself in your present job or starting an entirely new career, your self-confidence and positive attitude will increase your income.

Your fresh outlook will energize your work and stimulate your creativity. As you continue to boost your attitude daily, you will see that your optimism will soon lead you to improved income opportunities as well!

CHAPTER 15

The Millionaire Mindset Affirmations

I first learned about affirmations as a young child. My uncle, Baxter, would tell me, "I am as good as the next person--if I think I am." This belief has been with me for more than 25 years. And my favorite affirmation is from Brian Tracy, "You become what you think about the most." When I doubt myself, I quote affirmations and scriptures to be my highest self and elevate my mindset.

A millionaire mindset is one that takes as long as it takes to achieve and doesn't get deterred by setbacks. We grow this mindset with positive affirmations with daily repetition to reproduce whatever we tell ourselves. Such as affirmations that you won't fail no matter what, creating resilience and confidence to keep going even when things are tough.

Working with clients, sometimes I must encourage them to change how they speak about their situation and goals. Even though desires have not materialized, you must speak as though they will or have. Keep pursuing goals until you achieve yours. Mindset is a continuous process, and it is like breathing; you do it to live.

AFFIRMATION #1: _____

I Am Grateful for Money
I am 100% grateful for the money.

Money is neutral and what matters most is what I do with my money.

I achieve great good with the wealth I accumulate.

I am generous, big-hearted, and ready to help anyone in need. Wealth naturally flows to me, and as a result, I am grateful. I am grateful to my Creator for His abundant graces and generosity.

I know that the world is abundant, and I choose to receive that abundance.

I refuse to let past beliefs keep me from getting the wealth that I deserve.

I reject any myths that I have believed are unsupportive of my goals. I embrace my natural greatness and attract good things.

I make more than enough money.

When I make any money, I am filled with gratitude. I say, "Thank you," for even the smallest amounts of money, because gratitude fills me with joy and attracts more good things into my life. Money is a good thing and I make more than enough. I am a wealth magnet.

AFFIRMATION #2: _____

I Focus on Abundance

My mind is incredibly powerful.

What focuses on expands. What I give my attention to grows. My mind controls the outcomes that I experience in my life.

I have a mindset of abundance. I attract positive things because I constantly think about positive things. My outer life is extremely positive because my inner life is also extremely positive.

Because I focus on good things, I attract good things into my life.

I attract wealth, goodness, and beauty. I gratefully receive the abundance that the Creator provides me.

There is more than enough for every person in the world, including me, and I choose to receive what is rightfully mine.

Because I believe in abundance, I manifest abundance wherever I go and in whatever I do.

I know that my Creator has my back.

He is constantly looking for ways to bring good into my life. I must open myself up to the endless possibilities the Creator offers me. I live life to the fullest, enjoying and exploring all the amazing opportunities that come my way.

And because the Creator has my back, I am grateful.

I receive wealth and blessings with open hands, thankful for all that I am receiving.

AFFIRMATION #3: _____

I Act on My Dreams

Today, I choose to take massive action on my dreams. I know that when I combine my abundance mindset with massive action, I truly achieve limitless results. I avoid waiting for things to happen. I make them happen.

I am achieving my biggest dreams.

Nothing can stop me because I am relentless in pursuing them. I know the Creator has my back. This belief gives me great confidence as I pursue my goals and seek to accumulate wealth.

I am laser-focused on getting what I want because what I focus on becomes a reality.

I control all my thoughts and use them to push me toward achieving my dreams. My thoughts lead to my feelings, which lead to my actions, which lead to my reality.

I affirm that this is my financial best year so far. I hit all my financial goals. I attract the wealth that I desire and deserve. I am a financial success in every area of my life.

I know that I attract abundance, and when I combine abundance with action, amazing things happen.

I am excited to see all the good things happening in my life. I keep pushing and striving until I reach the desired success and my dreams come true. In summary, your affirmations will manifest because you think, speak and act as they already had and move toward the next goal. For instance, I have slayed my goals this week and the next weeks to come. You tell the subconscious mind what to think and it will because it knows no difference. In other words, you are the success that you live and show to the world. A dear friend of mine gave me the name "I am success," and I wear it proudly. So, friends, you are what you tell yourself.

PART IV
DIVERSIFICATION

Diversification helps manage risk by spreading investments across different asset classes, sectors, industries, and geographic regions. By diversifying your portfolio, you reduce the impact of any single investment's poor performance on your overall financial situation. If one investment performs poorly, others may offset the losses and provide stability. Capital preservation is vital for long-term financial goals such as retirement planning or funding your children's education. It is still crucial to carefully evaluate your investment choices, understand your risk tolerance, and periodically review and rebalance your portfolio to ensure it aligns with your financial goals and changing market conditions.

CHAPTER 16

Maximize Your Money and Prepare for Retirement Tips

After I gave a presentation on financial planning to a teacher's union, an older man approached me.

"I'm doing fine all by myself," he told me. He had a much higher annual income than most teachers because he had his teaching salary, as well as his salary from teaching in the after-school program and summer school. And he was controlling his spending and keeping his debt low. But when I heard the number he had for retirement, I paused.

"That number could be higher," I told him. "How many retirement accounts do you have?"

He had one.

I offered to meet with him to share some more options, but he was reluctant to work with me because I was a woman. Eventually, he took me up on a planning session, and he realized the value of my expertise.

Over a few years his portfolio grew to half a million dollars. Far higher than the average teacher's retirement savings. He's given me many referrals since then.

Some of you may feel like this teacher did—that you have a decent stash of cash and probably at least one 401K or Roth IRA account that's working for you. But that doesn't mean you've maxed out your investment revenue streams. When it comes to retirement, the earlier you plan and save, the better. Because of compound interest and tax deferrals, you can benefit more the earlier you start saving for retirement.

Do you know how much you need to save for retirement? How can you maximize your savings? In this chapter I share five things you can be doing to prepare for retirement.

Step 1

Think about the kind of retirement you want. Will you want to live differently when you retire? Start visualizing the type of lifestyle you want to live when you retire so you can tailor your savings goals to that lifestyle!

- How old do you want to be when you retire?
- Will you still work part-time?

- Where will you live? Do you want to live domestically or internationally?

- Will you be renting a house, or will you own your house?

- What will your monthly costs be?

- Will you care for you elderly parents?

- How much monthly retirement income do you want?

Step 2

Start saving today. Most (if not all) articles you read about retirement will encourage you to start saving today. The reason being is over time you can earn money from your savings via compound interest.

- Compound interest is the interest you earn on interest. It comes from reinvesting the interest you earn. It works in your favor.

- Hypothetical examples suggest that even a 25-year-old who invests $75 per month would accumulate more assets by 65-years-old compared to a 35-year-old who invests $100 per month.

- Put as much as you can away now so that you can reap the rewards later.

- Many financial experts recommend saving 15% -20% of your pre-tax income towards tax-advantaged accounts.

Step 3

Set a goal. Take time to carefully consider retirement expenses while factoring in inflation. Will you have other expenses that you might not have right now (such as children's expenses)?

- How much do you want to have when you retire (a lump sum amount)?

- Will you be traveling when you retire?

Step 4

Automate your savings to a retirement plan. Take advantage of tax deferrals to a retirement account. Set up automatic payments to your Individual Retirement Account (IRA) or 401(k). This way, the money gets deposited into your retirement savings plan before you think about it.

- 401(k)s have a high contribution limit ($22,500 if under age 50 (2023), and sometimes employers are willing to match your contributions. Check with your employer to see if they match what you put in.

- If you are under 50, you can contribute up to $6,500 to an IRA. If you are 50 or older, you can contribute up to $7,500 to an IRA (2023).

- Money contributed to a Traditional IRA may be deductible on your taxes that year. Then, when you withdraw money from that account in retirement, you pay taxes then.

- Money contributed to Roth IRAs is not deductible from your taxes that year. However, withdrawals you make from that account when in retirement are not taxed.

Step 5

Diversify your savings. Do not put all your eggs in one basket! Your IRA is just one piece of the puzzle. Consider investing in other assets, such as property, mutual funds, or bonds.

- Take advantage of employer matching. If your employer matches your IRA investments, take advantage of that! Deposit the maximum amount that your employer matches.

- Continually reduce your debt. Pay off your credit cards every month or pay as much as possible towards your credit card debt. When possible, accelerate your mortgage payments. As a rule of thumb, reduce your existing debt and avoid accumulating new debt.

Saving for your ideal lifestyle when you retire is a marathon, not a sprint. When you build your wealth over time, you don't have to worry about tackling everything all at once-

Remember that over time, your retirement account will build. Save at least 10-15% of your pretax income to start. You are already ahead of the game by thinking about this now so you can confidently retire on your terms.

CHAPTER 17

Index Funds and Hedge Funds

Some people are reluctant to invest in the stock market because of events like the housing bubble burst of 2008. Let me tell you how I helped my clients stay afloat. Finance professionals like me must communicate with clients in good and bad economic conditions, even though talking about losses is uncomfortable.

At the beginning of the 2008 stock market crash, I called all my clients to discuss their portfolio positions. One client, Missy, was traveling abroad at the time. She was invested largely in domestic Mutual Funds that were Index funds. For example, Dow Jones Industrial Average (DJIA), Russell Small Cap, Standard and Poor's (S&P) Mid Cap & 500.

She and I reviewed her current losses and options to help reduce further losses by moving her assets to stable funds like government bonds, money markets, and fixed-income mutual fund accounts. Missy trusted my advice and stopped the dwindling number in her retirement account. She continued contributing to that retirement account, but at a lower rate of return, without the greater risk of investing in the stock market by shifting to the bond market.

After the investment markets stabilized, we met and adjusted her investment allocations to invest a larger percentage in the stock market. By scheduling annual or semi-annual reviews with your finance coach, you are more prepared for the unexpected and can pivot quickly in a volatile market.

Missy was invested largely in index funds. During that bubble burst, there was a lot of conversation about hedge funds. I am frequently asked about hedge funds, and I'm not involved in any. Hedge funds are investment pools with limited partners (investors) contributing and are operated by a fund manager with specific goals of minimizing risk and maximizing returns. For example, BlackRock is the largest hedge fund in the world when you count assets under management (usabynumbers.com 5/23). Typically hedge funds are open to qualified investors, for instance, institutions. These funds are more expensive and riskier, so less of a safe bet for those planning for retirement.

Mutual Funds are somewhat similar to hedge funds, but they are different. An example of the largest mutual fund company in the world is The Vanguard Group, Inc. (finance yahoo.com, 5/23). You do not need to be an accredited investor with a specific net worth or income to invest, which is the case with a hedge fund. Also, they are often riskier investments than mutual funds and index funds. The hedge fund managers earn a larger profit from operating their funds from a percentage of the assets and about 20% of the fund's profits. Unlike a mutual fund manager's profit which is a percentage of the assets.

The dream of many investors is to build enough net worth to be able to invest in hedge funds. However, hedge funds frequently underperform index funds. These mystical funds can invest in just about anything, including complex derivatives. Such great flexibility and sophistication should ensure excellent results, but this is not always true.

There are many reasons to avoid hedge funds:

1. Hedge funds have extremely high fees. The managers are the only people who consistently profit from a hedge fund. The standard fee structure is 2% plus 20% of the profits. If the fund loses money, the managers are still paid. They also take a substantial chunk of any profits.

- If you've ever wondered why hedge fund managers are often billionaires, now you know.

- These fees are extremely hard to overcome. A 2% fee means you are already 2% behind. Losing 20% of your profits creates an additional burden.

- Keep in mind that many index funds have fees under 0.2%, and they keep their hands off your profits.

2. Hedge funds have become too big. While index funds are incredibly large, this is not an issue. Many hedge funds have become too big to take full advantage of lucrative financial opportunities. When a fantastic opportunity presents itself, the hedge fund can't put enough money into that opportunity to obtain the best return.

- Hedge funds must invest a sizable portion of the fund in lower-quality investments. The size of a fund can be incredibly challenging. Warren Buffett has often said he could earn 100% per year on a million dollars. Investing several billion dollars is very limiting.

3. The market is very efficient. This means that all the information available to investors has already been incorporated into the price of stocks. In theory, it is not possible to beat the market.

- The market is not 100% efficient since some investors regularly outperform the market. However, beating the market consistently is particularly challenging. To make up for that extra 2% fee, hedge funds must beat the market by more than 2%. That does not even take into account the 20% profit scrape.

- Hedge funds must beat the market by a considerable amount to provide a competitive return to an investor.

4. When hedge funds lose money, they can lose a lot. Hedge funds take on an elevated level of risk. Hedge funds managers love risk. They are already guaranteed 2%. Any profits greatly increase their income. A high level of risk is also necessary to overcome the fee structure and provide high returns to investors.

- The ratio of risk to returns is quite high.

- Hedge funds have a lot of exposure with margin accounts and short selling.

5. Low liquidity makes it difficult for investors to get out quickly. If the future is not looking bright, getting your investment out of the fund can take time. You might watch your investment shrink daily before you can cash out.

In contrast to hedge funds, index funds have many advantages. Index funds can provide comparable market returns with little of the risk found in hedge funds. The ability to guarantee market-matching returns with low fees can't be consistently matched by hedge funds.

You don't need a million dollars in net worth to invest in an index fund. Hedge funds cannot consistently beat the market and overcome the oppressive fee structure. Given the circumstances, the lowly index fund is an excellent investment for most investors.

Mutual funds let you pool your money with other investors to purchase stocks, bonds, and other securities. Mutual funds act as a basket of securities you buy all at once, which can help you diversify your portfolio. Actively managed mutual funds are more expensive; passively managed mutual funds are cheaper. These types of investments frequently used for retirement or long-term investors. Mutual funds allow investors to own diversified assets within a single investment.

Mutual funds pool investors' money to purchase stocks, bonds, and other assets. Mutual funds create a more diversified portfolio than most investors could on their own. Mutual funds are in the category of index funds, bond funds, and target-date funds. Investors do not own the stock, or the investments held by the fund, rather they share equally in the profits or losses of the funds total holding. Mutual funds are popular with investors who don't want to pick and choose individual investments themselves but want to benefit from the stock market's historically high average annual returns. A large majority of clients invest in mutual funds for retirement planning.

CHAPTER 18

Digital Currencies

Sometimes my clients ask me about adding cryptocurrency to their portfolios. I am not an expert in this space but will share what I understand. I believe that eventually, we will have digital currencies, and learning how Crypto and Blockchain function is wise. Crypto is still evolving, and everyone must do their due diligence before investing.

What is Cryptocurrency about? This is a common question these days among traditional and would-be investors. Cryptocurrency refers to digital or virtual currencies that use cryptography for security and operate independently of a central bank. The most well-known and widely used cryptocurrency is Bitcoin, created in 2009 by an anonymous person or group using the pseudonym name of Satoshi Nakamoto.

Cryptocurrencies are decentralized systems that rely on blockchain technology to record transactions and ensure their integrity. Blockchain is a distributed ledger that maintains a continuously growing list of records called blocks. Each block contains a timestamp and a link to the previous block, forming a chain of blocks.

The popularity of cryptocurrencies has grown significantly since the introduction of Bitcoin. Numerous other cryptocurrencies, often called altcoins, have emerged, each with unique features and purposes. Some notable altcoins include Ethereum, Ripple, Litecoin, and Bitcoin Cash.

Cryptocurrencies offer several potential advantages over traditional fiat currencies, including fast and secure transactions, lower fees, and greater accessibility. However, they also come with risks and challenges, such as price volatility, regulatory uncertainties, and potential security vulnerabilities.

Cryptocurrencies can be acquired through various means, including mining, where powerful computers solve complex mathematical problems to validate transactions and earn new coins as a reward. They can also be purchased on cryptocurrency exchanges using traditional fiat currencies or exchanged directly between individuals.

The future of cryptocurrencies is a topic of great interest and speculation. While it's challenging to predict with certainty, several trends and possibilities can be considered:

1. Increased Adoption: Cryptocurrencies have gained significant popularity and acceptance over the past decade. As more people become familiar with digital currencies and blockchain technology, adoption will continue growing. This could lead to increased mainstream acceptance and integration of cryptocurrencies into various industries and sectors, including finance, e-commerce, and governance.

2. Institutional Involvement: Institutional investors, such as hedge funds, asset management firms, and even traditional banks, have shown increasing interest in cryptocurrencies. Institutional involvement could bring more stability, liquidity, and legitimacy to the market, attracting a broader range of investors and potentially leading to more regulated frameworks.

3. Central Bank Digital Currencies (CBDCs): Many central banks worldwide are exploring issuing digital currencies. The respective central banks would back these CBDCs and could serve as a digital representation of fiat currencies. The introduction of CBDCs could have significant implications for the crypto space, potentially affecting the adoption and use of decentralized cryptocurrencies.

4. Regulatory Environment: Governments and regulatory bodies continuously evolve their approach to cryptocurrencies. While some countries have embraced cryptocurrencies and established favorable regulations, others have been more cautious or restrictive. The future regulatory landscape will play a crucial role in shaping the growth and development of cryptocurrencies.

5. Interoperability and Scalability: Cryptocurrencies face challenges related to scalability and interoperability. As the demand for digital currencies increases, efforts are being made to address these issues. Various projects focus on developing solutions that can enhance transaction speed, reduce fees, and improve cross-chain interoperability, which could further drive the adoption of cryptocurrencies.

6. Technological Advancements: Cryptocurrencies' underlying blockchain technology continues to evolve and improve. Innovations such as sidechains and layer-two solutions aim to address scalability and efficiency concerns. These technological advancements could lead to more robust and user-friendly cryptocurrencies, opening new possibilities for applications and use cases.

7. Environmental Concerns: The energy consumption associated with mining cryptocurrencies, particularly Bitcoin, has raised concerns about its environmental impact. As sustainability becomes a more prominent global issue, there may be a push for greener alternatives or the development of more energy-efficient consensus mechanisms.

In summary, here are a few points to consider when thinking about investing in cryptocurrencies:

1. Volatility: Cryptocurrencies are known for their high price volatility. The value of cryptocurrencies can fluctuate significantly in short periods, which can result in substantial gains or losses. It is essential to be prepared for this level of volatility and assess whether you can handle the potential financial risks involved.

2. Risk and Uncertainty: The cryptocurrency market is new and unpredictable. Regulatory changes, security vulnerabilities, technological developments, and market sentiment can all

impact the value and stability of cryptocurrencies. Understanding and evaluating the risks associated with investing in this emerging and evolving asset class is crucial.

3. Research and Education: Before investing in cryptocurrencies, you must conduct thorough research and gain a solid understanding of the technology, underlying principles, and the specific cryptocurrencies in which you are interested. Stay informed about market trends, news, and developments that could impact cryptocurrency.

4. Diversification: It is generally recommended to diversify your investment portfolio to manage risk. Cryptocurrencies can be highly volatile, so consider diversifying your investments across different asset classes, such as stocks, bonds, and real estate, to mitigate potential losses.

5. Long-Term Perspective: Cryptocurrency investments often require a long-term perspective. Short-term price fluctuations can be challenging to predict and time accurately. If you decide to invest, it's crucial to approach it with a long-term outlook and be prepared for potential volatility in the shorter term.

6. Professional Advice: If you need clarification on investing in cryptocurrencies or have limited knowledge and experience, consulting with a financial advisor or professional specializing in cryptocurrencies may be beneficial. They can provide personalized guidance based on your financial goals and risk tolerance.

CHAPTER 19

Precious Metals

Recently, I have been asked about investing in gold due to the current high inflation rates. Investing in precious metals, such as gold, silver, platinum, and palladium, is a popular option for diversifying investment portfolios and hedging against inflation or economic uncertainties. Here are some key points to consider when it comes to investing in precious metals:

1. Store of Value: Precious metals have been used as a store of value for centuries. They are tangible assets with intrinsic value (Intrinsic value is a measure of what an asset is worth.) and have historically maintained their worth over the long term. Gold is often considered a safe-haven asset during economic instability.

2. Diversification: Precious metals can provide diversification benefits to an investment portfolio. They often have a low correlation with other asset classes, such as stocks and bonds, meaning their value may not move in tandem with traditional investments. This can help reduce overall portfolio risk.

3. Inflation Hedge: Precious metals are often viewed as hedging against inflation. The value of paper currencies may decline during rising inflation, but the price of precious metals can rise. This can help preserve purchasing power and maintain the value of your investment.

4. Supply and Demand Dynamics: Supply and demand factors influence the prices of precious metals. While their supply is limited, demand can vary based on factors such as industrial usage, jewelry demand, investment demand, and central bank buying. Understanding these dynamics can help you assess potential price movements.

5. Different Investment Vehicles: There are several ways to invest in precious metals, including physical ownership, exchange-traded funds (ETFs), futures contracts, and mining stocks. Each option has advantages and considerations, such as storage costs, liquidity, and exposure to market fluctuations.

6. Risks and Volatility: While precious metals can stabilize an investment portfolio, they are not without risks. Precious metal prices can experience volatility, and their value may fluctuate over shorter periods. Having a long-term perspective and considering your investment horizon and risk tolerance is essential.

7. Research and Market Analysis: Before investing in precious metals, it's essential to conduct thorough research and stay informed about market trends, global economic conditions, and factors that can influence metal prices. Consult with a financial advisor or precious metals specialist to gain insights and make informed investment decisions.

It is important to note that investing in precious metals, like any investment, carries risks. The value of precious metals can go down and up, and past performance does not indicate future results. Consider your financial goals and risk tolerance and consult with professionals to determine if investing in precious metals aligns with your investment strategy.

Investing in precious metals can be done with both short-term and long-term perspectives, depending on your investment goals and time horizon. Here are some considerations for each approach:

1.   Short-Term Investing: Short-term investing in precious metals typically involves taking advantage of price fluctuations and market trends to generate profits over a brief period. Some strategies used in short-term investing include:

   a. Swing Trading: Traders aim to profit from short-term price movements by buying and selling precious metals within days or weeks.

   b. Technical Analysis: Short-term traders often rely on technical indicators and charts to identify patterns and make trading decisions based on short-term price movements.

   c. News and Events: Short-term investors may monitor economic news, geopolitical events, and central bank policies that can immediately impact precious metal prices.

Short-term investing in precious metals requires active monitoring of the market and a willingness to make frequent trades. It can be more speculative and carries a higher risk than long-term investing.

2.   Long-Term Investing: Long-term investing in precious metals involves holding onto your investment for an extended period, often years or even decades. Some reasons for long-term investing in precious metals include:

   a. Wealth Preservation: Precious metals, particularly gold, are often seen as a hedge against inflation and a way to preserve wealth over the long term. Holding precious metals can provide a store of value during economic downturns or periods of currency devaluation.

   b. Portfolio Diversification: Including precious metals in a long-term investment portfolio can help diversify risk. Precious metals often have a low correlation with other asset classes like stocks and bonds, which can provide a buffer against market volatility.

   c. Financial Stability: Long-term investors may view precious metals as a means of securing financial stability and protection against systemic risks or currency fluctuations.

Long-term investing in precious metals requires a patient approach and a focus on the fundamental factors influencing their value over time. It is essential to consider factors such as supply and demand dynamics, economic conditions, and geopolitical factors that can impact precious metal prices eventually.

Whether you choose short-term or long-term investing in precious metals, conducting thorough research is crucial, as understanding the market dynamics and aligning your investment strategy with your financial goals and risk tolerance.

CHAPTER 20

Important Financial Ratios

Over the years, many women clients and associates have told me, "I am no good with math or numbers." I would tell them that neither was I in elementary and middle school. The skill came to me when I began to apply myself to learn what I did not understand, and you can do the same.

There are so many financial ratios that knowing which matters the most is challenging. Understanding a few basic ratios will allow an investor to determine if additional scrutiny is warranted. Fortunately, all financial ratios use simple arithmetic learned by second grade. The key is understanding the message a particular ratio delivers.

The numerous financial ratios never reveal the entire story of a company, but much valuable information can be discovered and applied to make a final investment decision. Understand the most important financial ratios:

1. Price-to-Earnings Ratio (P/E). This is the price of a share of stock divided by the earnings per share of stock. It's the amount you'd be willing to pay for $1 of earnings.

    • If a share of a company's stock sells for $40 and the earnings are $2/share, the P/E would be 20. An investor who purchases this stock will earn $1 for every $20 invested.

2. Debt-to-Equity Ratio. The debt-to-equity ratio is a measure of the debt capital used by the company to finance its operations compared to the equity capital being used. If the ratio were 1.0, that would mean that the company's creditors theoretically have a claim to all the company's assets. Nothing would be left for the shareholders.

    • Debt-to-Equity Ratio (short-term debt + long-term debt) / shareholders' equity

3. Return on Equity (ROE). ROE is the amount of income the company generates against the amount of shareholder investments. It measures how efficiently shareholder investments are utilized to generate income.

    • ROE Net income/total shareholders' equity

4. Return on Assets (ROA). ROA is net income divided by total assets. It measures how effectively a company can turn its assets into income. For example, an office chair sitting in a closet is an asset, but it is not generating income for the business. The same applies to unnecessary equipment, marble lobbies, and other luxuries.

5. The Current Ratio measures a company's assets versus liabilities. A high ratio suggests that a company has plenty of cash and liquid assets to deal with bills. But it is essential to be careful and understand the high current ratio. A stockpile of unsold inventory can raise the ratio and be a sign of trouble.

   • A low current ratio suggests that the company could struggle to meet its short-term liabilities and suffer from a cash shortage.

6. Net Profit Margin is calculated by dividing the net income by the net revenue. This is the amount of profit generated by each dollar of sales. Some companies make much more profit per $1 of sales than others. Real estate and health care are often mentioned as industries with high-profit margins.

7. Dividend Yield is the dividend-price ratio and = (dividend per share/price per share). Investors can view dividend payments as a cash flow to investors. Companies with a higher dividend yield have the potential to be more attractive to investors than those with lower yields.

Financial ratios are not just for financial professionals. Understanding financial ratios is necessary to invest in stocks if you are researching. They provide a quick view of a company's financial status and future. It is impossible to successfully make investing decisions with financial ratios alone, but these ratios are an excellent place to start.

CHAPTER 21

Working with a Finance Coach

Working with a finance coach can offer several benefits and be a worthwhile investment for individuals seeking to improve their financial situation. Here are some reasons why you should consider working with a finance coach such as myself:

1. Objective guidance: A finance coach provides an outside perspective on your finances. They can assess your current situation, identify areas for improvement, and help you set realistic financial goals. Their objectivity allows them to offer unbiased advice tailored to your specific needs.

2. Personalized approach: A coach works closely with you to understand your financial goals, values, and challenges. They can create a customized plan that aligns with your unique circumstances and aspirations. This personalized approach ensures you receive tailored strategies and recommendations to address your financial concerns.

3. Knowledge and expertise: Finance coaches are professionals with expertise in personal finance. They deeply understand financial concepts, strategies, and best practices. Their knowledge can help you navigate complex financial matters, such as budgeting, investing, debt management, tax planning, and retirement planning. You can make informed decisions and optimize your financial outcomes by leveraging their expertise.

4. Accountability and motivation: One of the significant advantages of working with a finance coach is the built-in accountability they provide. They can hold you responsible for sticking to your financial plans, tracking your progress, and making necessary adjustments. Moreover, they serve as a source of motivation and encouragement, helping you stay focused on your goals during challenging times.

5. Education and empowerment: A coach helps you manage your finances and aims to educate and empower you to make better financial decisions independently. They can teach you valuable financial skills, improve your financial literacy, and provide tools and resources to enhance your financial knowledge. This knowledge equips you with the confidence and competence to take control of your financial future.

6. Overcoming behavioral biases: Many individuals face behavioral biases regarding money management, such as emotional spending, impulsive decision-making, or fear of investing. A finance coach can help you recognize and overcome these biases, guiding how to make rational and informed financial choices. They can support you in developing healthy financial habits and behaviors that lead to long-term financial success.

7. Time and money savings: Although working with a finance coach typically involves a financial commitment, it can ultimately save you time and money in the long run. By receiving expert guidance, you can avoid costly mistakes, optimize your financial strategies, and use your resources more efficiently. The financial knowledge and skills you gain through coaching can continue to benefit you throughout your life.

When choosing a coach, consider their qualifications, experience, and reputation. Look for someone who aligns with your values and understands your financial goals. This is important.

Finding a good fit in a finance coach depends on your specific needs and preferences. Here are a few factors to consider when evaluating potential finance coaches:

1. Experience and qualifications: Consider the coach's professional background and credentials. Look for certifications such as Certified Financial Planner (CFP), Chartered Financial Consultant (ChFC), Certified Fund Specialist (CFS), or Chartered Financial Analyst (CFA). Additionally, consider their years of experience working with clients in similar situations to yours.

2. Communication style: Pay attention to the coach's communication style and whether it resonates with you. Effective communication is essential for building a solid working relationship. Some people prefer a direct and no-nonsense coach, while others prefer a more supportive and empathetic approach. Choose a coach whose communication style makes you feel comfortable and understood.

3. Compatibility: Finding a coach with whom you feel comfortable and connected is essential. A good fit involves trust, open communication, and mutual understanding. During an initial consultation or interview, note how well you connect with the coach and whether you feel they genuinely understand your financial goals and concerns.

4. Reviews and recommendations: Seek feedback from others who have worked with your chosen coach. Check for reviews, testimonials, or recommendations from previous clients. This can provide insights into the coach's effectiveness, professionalism, and overall satisfaction of their clients.

5. Cost and value: Consider the coach's fees and whether they align with your budget. While cost is a factor, it's essential to prioritize the value you expect to gain from working with the coach. A skilled coach who can significantly improve your financial situation may be worth the investment, but ensure the fees are reasonable and proportionate to the services provided.

Remember to interview multiple coaches, ask questions, and compare their offerings before deciding. A good fit ultimately depends on your preferences, goals, and comfort level with the coach.

Finance coaches can offer various services to help individuals with their financial goals and challenges. Here are some standard offerings you might find from finance coaches:

1. Financial planning: Finance coaches can assist in creating comprehensive financial plans tailored to your specific circumstances. They can help you set realistic goals, develop strategies, and create a roadmap for your financial future.

2. Budgeting and cash flow management: Coaches can help you develop effective budgeting techniques and strategies to better manage your income and expenses. They can work with you to create a personalized budget, track your spending, and identify areas where you can save or make adjustments.

3. Debt management: If you're struggling with debt, a financial coach can guide how to tackle it effectively. They can help you understand different debt repayment strategies, negotiate with creditors, and develop a plan to reduce and eventually eliminate your debt.

4. Investment guidance: Coaches can offer insights and advice on investment options based on your risk tolerance, financial goals, and time horizon. They can help you understand different investment vehicles, evaluate opportunities, and build a diversified investment portfolio aligned with your objectives.

5. Retirement planning: Finance coaches can assist in creating retirement plans, helping you estimate the amount you'll need to save for retirement, exploring different retirement account options, and strategizing to achieve your desired retirement lifestyle.

6. Tax planning: Coaches can help you optimize your tax strategies by identifying deductions, credits, and other tax-saving opportunities. They can guide tax-efficient investing, retirement contributions, and other tactics to minimize your tax liability.

7. Financial education and literacy: Many finance coaches prioritize financial education. They can teach you fundamental financial concepts, improve your financial literacy, and equip you with the knowledge and skills to make informed financial decisions independently.

8. Accountability and ongoing support: Coaches can provide ongoing support to keep you accountable for your financial goals. They can review your progress, offer guidance during challenging times, and motivate you to stay on track.

Conclusion

" Imagine, Believe and Prosper" a guide to financial success, is just like becoming mentally and physically fit; it is the ability to deal well with an adverse circumstance by coping with challenging times. We all need a financial alignment in life. We are coping with the effects of the Covid- 19 Pandemic that transformed the world and the 2023 economic uncertainties of a recession. Many people suffered the devastation of losing loved ones unexpectedly, losing employment, homes, and even having mental health issues. People's savings, investment accounts, and retirement plans became ATMs for withdrawals. Some people had to deplete some of these accounts to keep their households afloat. The practice of having an emergency fund rang true then and in the future. Financial Planning is the key that can help you in your darkest hours to survive the worst of times. Yeah, we learned firsthand the importance of utilizing and applying financial success.

The starting point of any responsibility is practicing initiative-taking money management techniques that will assist and determine the state of your finances. In times of trouble, we need to get back to the basics, a firm foundation that will help us weather economic storms. Even without economic uncertainty, this knowledge is essential to have and practice. Put our trust in the Creator and learn everything about finances; incorporate these principles daily and share the information with others. Therefore, we will have peace amid any storm or circumstance.

As a reminder, trouble does not always last. If you are experiencing some challenges, know your financial circumstance will not grow stagnant; it will thrive and grow. Use your strategic plan to climb to the level of your goals. You must have a target in front of you to aim at. Exercise your muscles daily to strengthen your outlook on life and acquire your goals. Always seek to be the best version of yourself by challenging yourself and continuously practicing self-development. Finally, review your action steps, monitor your growth achievements, and celebrate your accomplishments regularly. Yeah, celebrate you. Hold yourself accountable for your success.

When I recite this mantra, Imagine, Believe, and Prosper ®, to everyone, it means this. If you can think and visualize your desires, this is to Imagine. Lay the foundation of a strong belief mindset without doubting; have faith in your goals and dreams; this is to Believe. Reap the benefits and rewards of what you planned, sacrificed, and worked earnestly to obtain; you have earned the rite of passage to Prosper financially with love, peace, joy, and happiness.

My current journey takes me to my latest project, hosting the Wealth Legacy Retreat (WLR) business conference in Atlanta, Georgia, in September 2023. This luxury two-day wealth conference will address financial and estate planning, tax planning, insurance, entrepreneurship, access to capital, real estate, construction, health and wellness, art collecting, self-development, and more from the subject matter expert's experience. Sharing knowledge, experience, and resources in this perfect intimate retreat-like setting is ideal for attendees to gather, learn, meet, mingle, and connect with others to discuss these critical subjects.

The WLR will bring a unique conference to many entrepreneurs to assist in building and expanding their legacy with the appropriate resources. We will delight in serving attendees and provide this amazing opportunity of a one-stop-shop of related topics and tools to assist them in expanding their most tremendous success. The WLR is dedicated to assisting everyone with their financial security, personal development, legacy, and peace of mind. I earnestly desire that when the attendees depart from this event, they will be presented with tools for a plan of action that transforms their life's purpose and passion. "We spend a great portion of our life working to acquire wealth, to share and enjoy with others, which is key to building a legacy that passes on forever in people's hearts, minds, and souls. It is good and equally significant to leave a great inheritance to your loved ones." – Gloria S. Riley.

Now you go and Imagine, Believe and Prosper ®.

APPENDIX

Bonus Worksheets: Planning Your Budget

HOUSEHOLD BUDGET

Gross Monthly Income

Salary 1 $ _____

Salary 2 $ _____

Other Income* $ _____

Total Monthly Income $ _____

*Other monthly income includes hobbies, interest, investment, child support/alimony, and extra money. This income may change from month to month or year to year.

Being able to manage your income will help you to know which expenses to give a higher-paying priority to and how much income is available for taxes, savings, and spending. Another benefit is that it should help keep you out of debt. The following worksheets for Monthly expenses, Personal financial statements, and Debts will help you to budget well while tracking your progress.

Budget Data Sheets

Budget Data Entry

Salary					
Pension/Retirement					
Social Security					
Annuities					
Stocks/Bonds					
Tax Return					
Other					
Income Tax Deduction (Federal + State)					
Other					
Real Estate Taxes					
HOA Dues					
Electric					
Garbage					
Water					
Sewer					
Natural Gas					
Cable					
Internet					
Cellular Phone					
Home Phone					
Security System					
Home Improvement					
Furniture					
Yard maintenance/Gard					
Furniture					
House Mortgage (P&I)					
Auto Loans					
Boat Loans					
Credit Card					

Budget Data Entry

RV/Camping Trailer					
Student Loan					
Alimony					
Child Support					
Groceries					
Restaurants					
Spending Cash					
Haircuts/Nails/Massages					
Dry Cleaning					
Pet Food & Medication					
Gym Membership					
Clothes & Shoes					
Chiropractor					
Auto Insurance					
Homeowners Insurance					
Health Insurance					
Dental Insurance					
Life Insurance					
Long Term Care Insurance					
Medical Supplements					
Vision & eyecare					
Medications					
Annual Tune Up					
Fuel					
Oil Change(s)					
Maintenance					
Tires					
Repairs					
Memberships					
License Renewals Tabs					
Public Transportation					

Budget Data Entry

Vacations					
Birthdays					
Christmas					
Anniversary					
Amazon Prime					
Hobbies & Lessons					
Magazines & Newspapers					
Software Subscriptions					
Netflix					
Movie Rentals					
Tithes & Offerings					
Missions					
Charitable Donation					
Financial Adviser					
Tax Preparation					

"Precious treasure and oil are in a wise man's dwelling, but a foolish man devours it."
Proverbs 1:20.

Total expenses paid $ _____

Income vs. Living Expenses:

Total Monthly Income $ _____

Minus Total Monthly

Expense $ _____

Monthly Surplus or Deficit* $ _____

* Keep track of your spending and income regularly, and if you have a deficit, you need to make adjustments in your budget items that are the root cause. Keep good receipts of your spending in a folder for handy use. Some months of monitoring may be better than others; nevertheless, keep fine-tuning the budget.

PERSONAL FINANCIAL STATEMENT

Assets (Present Market Value*)	Amount
Cash/ Checking/Savings	
Stocks/ Bonds/Gold	
IRA	
Cash Value of Life Insurance	
Pension/ Retirement	
Home	
Other Real Estate Investments	
Business Value	
Vehicles	
Furniture	
Jewelry	
Total Assets	

These figures will come from your Budget Data Sheet.

The Present Market Value is the current value of the assets if the assets were liquidated or sold today at the current value. For instance, you purchased a vehicle a couple of years ago cost $25,000; if you sell the same vehicle today, valued at $10,000, this is the Present Market Value.

Keep great records, receipts, statements, and reports of your assets because values change, and you always want to know the current value. This information is helpful to share when seeking a loan or other financing.

Liabilities (Current Debt*)

Credit Card	
Automobile Loans	
Home Mortgage	
Other Real Estate Mortgages	
Personal Debt to Relatives/Friends	
Business Loans	
Medical Bills	
Past Due Bills	
Life Insurance Loans	
Bank Loans	
Other Debt or Loans	
Total Liabilities	

These figures will come from your Budget Data Sheet.

Net Worth (Assets minus Liabilities) $ _____

The value of all your assets owned minus the value of liabilities you owe.   For example, if you are paying a car loan, this is a liability, not an asset. This is an asset if the car is paid in full and you own the title.

Debt is an obligation of money that the debtor owes to the creditors. A debt is an arrangement with a creditor where the individual makes a large purchase that they could not afford at one time and agrees to deferred payments over time.

DEBT LIST

Creditor	Interest Rate	Monthly Payment	Balance Due

Use this list to monitor your debt, negotiate interest rates, reduce the use of debt, and devise a plan to pay off balances sooner rather than later.

DEBT TO INCOME RATIO WORKSHEET

MONTHLY GROSS INCOME (annual income ÷ by 12) $ _____

MONTHLY CREDIT OBLIGATIONS

Rent/Mortgage $ _____

Auto loan payment $ _____

Student loan $ _____

Credit card (minimum) $ _____

Other loans payments $ _____

Child support $ _____

Total $ _____

Monthly Gross Income x 28%= $ _____

(Maximum income to support new debt)

Monthly Gross Income x 36% =

(Maximum income to support new debt and existing debt) $ _____

These figures will come from your Budget Data Sheet.

Example: MONTHLY CREDIT OBLIGATIONS

MONTHLY GROSS INCOME ($67,521 annual income ÷ by 12) $ 5,626.75

Rent/Mortgage $1,275.00

Auto loan payment $ 488.00

Student loan $ 298.00

Credit card (minimum)

                                                         $ 110.50

Other loans payments

Child support

                                                         $ 430.00

Total

                                                         $3,025.25

Monthly Gross Income x 28%= $1,575.40

(Maximum income to support new debt)

Monthly Gross Income x 36% =

(Maximum income to support new debt and existing debt) $2,025.63